SECRETS AND SCUDS

By

James "Doc" Crabtree

D1519233

Dedicated to the memory of James Brown,

one of the 146 Americans who

were casualties from Desert Shield

and Desert Storm.

PREVIEWS OF THINGS TO COME:

1990

TABLE OF CONTENTS

INTRODUCTION

Desert Storm was more than a conflict, it was an experience. Or at least it was for me and my fellow soldiers. Trained to fight the Soviets in a bitter, all-out slugging match, we found ourselves instead in the Middle East (although it was accepted at the time as another potential theater for WWIII), fighting an enemy shooting at us with rockets which were just one step up from Hitler's V2s, listening to enemy propaganda broadcasts which were not just unconvincing but ridiculous and dealing with equipment which was falling apart thanks to Army bureaucracy. Oh, and there was the whole secret-weapon thing. We saw all of this and more.

It was March 5th, 1991. The place: southern Iraq, well north of the Saudi border.

Our vehicle, a CUCV "Blazer," pulled up to the base of a hill. Private First Class Wailikanan shut off the engine and I stepped out. Sergeant Seipel elected to stay in the vehicle; after his recent brush with an Iraqi mine you really couldn't blame him.

Like a typical American tourist I had my camera out, but it wasn't some roadside marker or scenic overlook I was taking photographing. Instead I was taking pictures of the remnants of Saddam's army, the team that only scored second-place in the recent Middle Eastern Championships. But unfortunately for Saddam, second place was also last.

Ex-Soviet S60 antiaircraft guns sat on top of the hill. The guns were not damaged by any of the many Coalition airstrikes. They had not run out of ammunition, which was still stacked in nearby bunkers. They were not sabotaged by the Iraqis, who had taken off at some point and were almost certainly in a POW enclosure somewhere. They had not even been fired, or else there would have been spent ammunition casings.

The guns were simply there.

Clouds of smoke dotted the horizon, but by now combat was over. The smoke came from French and U.S. Army engineers who were destroying anything not knocked out during the air campaign, damaged in the rare instances of Iraqi resistance, or "souvenired to death" following the cease-fire announcement. So if it hadn't been bombed, shot, or looted it wasn't going to be left behind for Saddam's army. If the madman wanted to cause trouble again, he was going to have to start from scratch.

I took photos. Even while we were there, a French patrol pulled up and began examining another part of the antiaircraft site. I took a few last pictures as this site was almost certainly about to go up in smoke as well.

But we won. And I was there first-hand and at ground level to see how it happened. I went from reading history to living it. But the road to this little spot in Iraq was a long one...

1. GET READY...

"Air Defense Artillery" is a confusing name. It used to be Antiaircraft Artillery, back when the U.S. Army used big antiaircraft guns to shoot down airplanes, but the abbreviation (AAA, or "Triple-A") seemed bland and the service was always getting mixed up with that organization that tries to help motorists get their cars towed. Besides, guns were passé... everyone knew the future of shooting down airplanes lay in missiles, not flak. Why shoot hundreds of thousands of shells in the hopes of hitting an enemy plane when a single missile could, under the right circumstances, take down an enemy plane every time? The artillery thing was probably left in as part of Army tradition... or more likely due to a lack of imagination.

I joined the Army, after it got rid of that "we-do-more-before-nine-a.m.-than-most-people-do-all-day" recruiting campaign. That sounded exhausting! They switched to "Be all that you can be." The recruiter showed me pictures of these big Hawk missiles which were designed to take out Soviet warplanes. I LIKED the idea of shooting down Soviet warplanes. I liked the idea of shooting down airplanes in general... something about being denied an opportunity to become a pilot because I wore glasses.

I found out that I was good at the technical side of my job, although I was never a perfect fit for the Army. I could learn how to take apart and put a rifle back together again after one demonstration, but I had difficulty in dealing with the bureaucracy and contradictions of the service. My cartooning provided an outlet. I was also a bit of a jinx; I scared a bunch of Rangers whom I was driving in a truck once, crushed a Mercedes in Germany and had a Patriot launcher malfunction on me and try to raise itself to launch position on its own initiative.

My personal emblem became a playing card with Thirteen Hearts on it and the motto "Unlucky to Some." I should have had it tattooed on my arm but I settled for having it painted on my jacket.

So what happened? The Army gave me an opportunity to become an officer. After a short stint as an ROTC cadet and an even shorter stint in the Ohio National Guard I found myself on active duty again.

I was at Fort Bliss, Texas on August 2nd 1990 watching CNN and seeing the invasion of Kuwait unfold live. Iraq's occupation of Kuwait would become notoriously brutal. Worse, Saddam[1] now had both his own oilfields and Kuwait's

1

and those of Saudi Arabia were just a few hours' drive by tank. Obviously, something would have to be done.

For my unit it was another Thursday. I was currently assigned to "B" Battery, 2nd Battalion, 1st ADA Regiment. My unit was equipped with the Hawk surface-to-air missile system, which I was familiar with from my previous tour in the Army spent as a private[2].

We weren't exactly on alert but we weren't exactly doing business as usual either. 11th Air Defense Brigade, to which our battalion belonged, advised all officers to remain close to the phones, just in case. Rumors were running wild: the 82nd Airborne was already on the ground in Saudi Arabia, Iraqi saboteurs had stolen a computer from a Patriot unit in the desert, Saddam Hussein was seen shopping at the Cielo Vista Mall... it wouldn't be long before the post newspaper and the chain of command would be clamping down on operational security.

Some Army units are better than others and I was fortunate to be in one of the best. We had some excellent officers: Captain Charles Fletcher, our battery commander, who was a West Point grad but more concerned more with results than making sure everything was "dress-right-dress." 1st Lieutenant Joe Pace, our Executive Officer, who was from Alaska and who worked hard to make sure the officers got the training they needed. 2nd Lieutenant Ron Williams, platoon leader for 2nd Platoon and probably the best lieutenant in the entire battalion. Initially I was assigned to work for Lt. Williams. Lieutenant Whitmire, Lieutenant Riley and Chief Dungy, all great guys, completed our complement of officers.

Patriot units were alerted. We prepared our equipment too, since our missile system could compensate for Patriot's Achilles Heel, i.e. its inability to"see" and engage enemy aircraft in a full circle.[3] Sooner or later we felt sure we would be alerted for overseas movement as well. By the end of the first day we were told that 2nd Battalion, 7th ADA (Patriot) was being airlifted that night to go to Saudi Arabia. Its batteries would be positioned to defend ports and airfields from air or missile attack.

We didn't know it at the time, but there was considerable discussion as to which Air Defense units would be going and what role they would play.

---

[1] Will Rogers once stated that he "never met a man he didn't like." Documentary evidence proves he never met Saddam Hussein.

[2] Actually, I started out as a Private E-2, was a PFC before long and a Specialist-4 before I applied for an active-duty ROTC scholarship.

[3] Raytheon finally came up with a radar design which can provide Patriot with a limited 360-degree capability... in 2014. Better late than never.

The officers of Bravo Battery, 2nd Battalion, 1st Air Defense
Artillery. From left to right, rear row: Lt. Williams, Cpt. Fletcher,
Chief Dungy, Lt. Riley. Front row: Lt. Whitmire, Lt. Rich, Lt.
Crabtree, Lt. Pace.

The "Peace Train," its loading complete and ready for shipment by
rail to the Gulf of Mexico and onward by ship to Saudi Arabia. The
loading of the train was grueling and frustrating for the crews.

Initially the higher-ups talked about shipping us with just three live missiles to Saudi Arabia and we would worry about where to get more later. Or that the battalion would be sent to support the Marines but only with a battery's worth of trucks, which would severely restrict our mobility. Or that we would be leaving soon to defend Turkey, which I didn't even know needed defending. I suppose we should have counted ourselves lucky... I know of at least one ADA unit which was deployed with a bunch of former East German trucks and spent their time moving freight. [4]

And with all this activity going on, we were told to tell people outside the unit that we were merely conducting an Emergency Deployment Readiness Exercise... and that it was just coincidental that it was coming at the same time as the biggest military build-up our country had seen since Vietnam.

We spent the next two months simply getting ready. This was in contrast to how we were trained... we were supposed to be among the first units to go overseas, but it seemed as if the Big Plan was being tinkered with on a daily basis. Instead of going over fast we would go slow, following only after the Patriots and ground units capable of holding up Saddam's war machine arrived in Saudi Arabia. This was Operation Desert Shield, and the Coalition formed by President George H.W. Bush would see many other countries rush forward to help.

With Desert Shield picking up speed, Captain Fletcher made the decision to remain as the BC, even though he was scheduled to relinquish command. On the other hand, we replaced several of our senior NCOs with volunteers from the 6th ADA Brigade, which is normally a training unit and not deployable. Sergeant First Class Hurt and Staff Sergeants Tijerina and Mitchell would prove to be excellent replacements for some of our "non-deployables." They knew the technical side of their job and were no-nonsense types. Mitchell and Tijerina had both served in the Marine Corps in Vietnam and liked to say that "the best Army sergeant is a Marine."

Meanwhile, public support for the mission was swift and direct. Voices of anti-Saddam outrage seem to drown out the campus peaceniks and liberal apologists in the United States. Enthusiasm for the military was also expressed in many forms and would continue during the days ahead.

Everyone won. Americans could express their love of their country again without fear of ridicule and former hippies and hippie wannabes could relive the sixties. I heard a rumor that morons even called some folks at the base asking where they could get draft cards... so they could burn them. In all fairness, these

---

[4] 3rd Battalion, 2nd ADA got this job. In only made sense: we needed supply trucks more than we needed close-range air defense.

might have been younger morons who were not aware that we had replaced the draftee Army with the all-volunteer Army in the 1970s.

Iraq's high-handed taking of hostages and its brutal occupation of Kuwait would result in United Nation's sanctions and resolutions[5] which eventually gave the Coalition of countries opposed to Saddam the legal basis for attacking him and liberating Kuwait. Later some countries would claim that while they had voted for legal sanctions against Iraq it was *illegal* to actually enforce them.

We modified some of our vehicles with wooden shelters so they could be used as mobile buildings. The vehicles and equipment were also painted a light tan, or sand color. We took advantage of the new paint job to add a stencil on them: a palm tree with an ADA branch insignia. Other deploying units did the same, although in all cases bumpers kept the official unit designations on them.

Hard decisions were finally made, though. Our unit was to deploy as part of an "electronic task force," an ad hoc units consisting of the entire 2nd Battalion 1st ADA, "A," "B" and "E" Patriot Batteries of 3rd Battalion, 43rd ADA, and the ICC (Information Coordination Central) from 1st Battalion, 43rd ADA. The ICC was a command and control van which would allow us to operate a network of both Patriot and Hawk units together. It would make it possible for the Patriot missile batteries to concentrate on scud missile attacks while our Hawk fire platoons protected them from attacks from the Iraqi Air Force. We would also provide a "point defense" for areas of particular importance, such as seaports and airports. In addition, we were to protect XVIII Airborne Corps and the tens of thousands of Soldiers being gathered to its colors from enemy attack from the air. The name of our ad hoc unit was ask Force Scorpion.

Prospects for war with Iraq weren't pleasant. Saddam had made it abundantly clear that he would really like to have nuclear weapons, but was so far unable to do anything about it. What he COULD make was chemical weapons. He used them on the Iranians during the Iran-Iraq War and for good measure used them on the Kurds... just in case they were thinking of starting any trouble. We took THAT threat very seriously and were constantly training with our protective masks and other gear.

---

[5] Resolutions 660, 661, 662, 664, 665, 666, 667, 669, 670, 674, 677, and 678. Not that Saddam seemed to be keeping count.

INVASION!

**SADDAM MANAGES TO BRING HIS
BRAND OF FASCISM TO THE TINY
STATE OF KUWAIT**

But even as we worked hard to improve our proficiency on the missile system and get ready for a chemical attack we also improved other fighting skills, such as pistol shooting. We had a shooting competition at the Rod and Gun Club, with each of us firing our newly-issued 9mm Beretta automatics. Even the battalion chaplain got in on the act, engaging targets in full SWAT mode.

I fired a few rounds to get oriented to the 9mm. Then the competition started. Unfortunately I got some bad reloads and I had a round get lodged in the barrel. It was a good thing Lieutenant Pace had been coaching me or else I might have seriously injured my hand by firing into a jammed barrel.

And so it turned out that when the scores were tallied up I came in last place. Why? Because I had only fired a few rounds into the target before my pistol jammed. Even the worst shot among us had managed to score more points than I did. However, in what passes for Army humor, the competition didn't just have trophies for 1st, 2nd and 3rd Place; they also had one for LAST Place. And so I was awarded a trophy with an equine rear end. In front of the entire battalion as they stood in formation.

So my pistol jams and I get a horse's ass trophy? I guess in some twisted way that is logical... if your weapon fails you in combat then you will definitely come in last place. It doesn't matter if it's your fault or not. Still, I might have asked for PROOF that I came in last... whatever happened to my DA88-R, Combat Pistol Qualification Scorecard?

We had classes on what to do if we were made prisoners of war. We watched films of former Vietnam War Soldiers who were captured and then held in harsh conditions of captivity. We had some speakers come out to address our unit as well. It seemed pretty unlikely to me that someone in our unit would be captured by the Iraqis if a real war broke out in the Middle East, but you never know. At least in this way we had some preparation.[6]

We were finally issued Desert Combat Uniforms, or DCUs, added via a DA3645, Additional Organizational Clothing and Individual Equipment Record. None of us had ever even SEEN desert uniforms, or even knew they existed before Saddam's Great Miscalculation. The uniform pattern would get the nickname "chocolate chip" because of the mix of dark spots in it. Not everyone got complete uniforms right away, apparently because some sizes weren't available. And no one made desert-colored insignia for them either so we put the forest-green versions put on instead.

---

[6] Specialist Melissa Coleman and Specialist David Lockett, both Soldiers from the 233rd Transportation Company based at Fort Bliss, would in fact be captured during Desert Storm when they got lost near the Iraqi border.

Our personnel processing went along as well. Our yellow immunization records (PHS-731) were updated as we got shots, including a brand-new one for anthrax. Our Servicemembers Group Life Insurance (SGLI) information was updated on our SGLV 8283 forms and so were our wills. They also checked our teeth. God forbid we should get shot AND have gingivitis.

Finally, in the middle of September, we had the opportunity to road-march the equipment and load it on a train so it could be shipped to the Gulf of Mexico and then placed on a ship. It was royal pain to both train to load *and* load a train at the same time. Our road-weary equipment arrived at the railhead and each machine had to be driven up a ramp, towing its piece of the Hawk missile system behind it. Or sometimes NOT its piece of equipment, since things were reorganized to use up every foot of space possible on the cars, regardless of the system's normal configuration. Tools and other equipment were in short supply, slowing down work. And of course, this was Texas so the Sun was doing its worst to us as we tried to get the job done. It took a full day to get the entire battalion loaded.

Our trucks were really bad. They were Vietnam-era machines, and the Army, in its wisdom, was reluctant to provide new parts for them. It seems that at some point our unit was to be converted to Patriot, so the Army didn't see any point in keeping the old trucks running when we could get completely new ones later. The only problem was we had to go to Saudi Arabia with the old ones. There was a rumor that got our hopes up... our unit would receive new trucks from pre-positioned stocks in the Middle East, in order to replace the worst of our vehicles. This would turn out to be a cruel lie.

If we needed new trucks we were also still short of soldiers, for various reasons. The NCOs from 6th ADA Brigade were a great addition but we had personnel who couldn't deploy due to medical issues and other problems and we could sure use qualified personnel.

This led to an incident that happened after the "Peace Train" left with our Hawk missiles. All of us officers were hanging around Lt. Pace's office when a sergeant who Pace knew from another unit stopped by.

"Yeah, I sure wish I could go over there with you guys," the man lamented, "but as long as I'm in 1-43 I'll never get to go to Saudi."

Pace responded with his typical enthusiasm. "Hey, I might be able to help." He pulled out one of the papers on his cluttered desk. "This latest policy letter gives me the authority to pull NCOs if we have a critical shortage. Didn't you used to be a Hawk radar mechanic?"

The man's relaxed attitude went away as if someone had pushed an "off" button. "Well, yeah..."

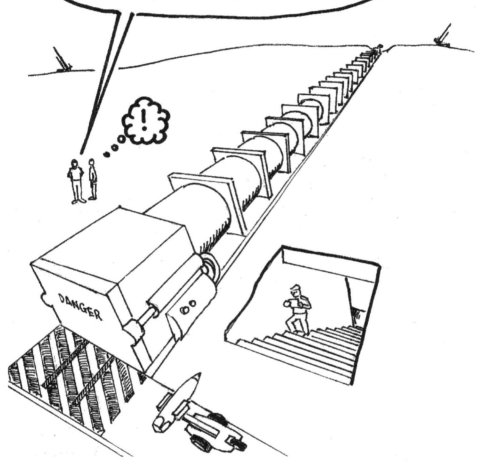

SADDAM'S
BIG BABYLON
PROJECT

9

"No problem. We're short a 24 Romeo right now."

He gave a short, nervous laugh. "Oh, well my commander would never approve..."

"He wouldn't have a choice," Pace continued. "It's policy. All you have to do is fill out a DA 1610 Personnel Action Form..."

Now the sergeant was sweating a little bit, and it wasn't just from the heat. "Uh, I'd like to, but I'd have to leave my family and everything." He headed for the door. "Thanks for the offer, though!"

Joe shook his head after the man was gone. "I thought he was really gung-ho but I guess a person's true colors come out when there's a chance you might get killed."

Lieutenant "Wally" Whitmire suddenly perked up from his corner of the office and asked in his southern drawl "WHO-all could get killed?!"

Joe feigned surprise. "Haven't you been watching the news lately? WE-all could get killed!"

Iraq had spent most of the 1980s fighting their next-door neighbors, the Iranians. Apparently Saddam made the same mistake Hitler did with the USSR: he thought that the Iranian military would be a walkover because of recent purges by that country's civilian leadership. Or maybe he calculated that the chances of his army floundering in snowstorms were minimal. In any case, what better time to take control of the Iranian province of Arabistan, which contained oilfields and oil shipping facilities, than during Iran's diplomatic isolation following the American hostage crisis?

But the Iran-Iraq War had the distinction of being fought between two oil-rich countries, both of which had the means to buy high-tech weapons with little regard to the economic needs of their respective populations. The war saw Iranian human-wave attacks, Iraqi use of gas, and even the use of tactical ballistic missiles by both sides during what was called the "War of the Cities," which resulted in Tehran and Baghdad getting involuntary urban renewal by the occasional scud. The war ended in 1988 and both sides were in bad shape.

Saddam had a big army that he couldn't afford to keep and he couldn't afford to demobilize, as dumping unemployed soldiers would badly damage an already weak postwar economy. So what did he do? He invaded his next-door neighbor, Kuwait. While Kuwait might have assisted the Iraqis during the Iran-Iraq War with money and other aid, it had a miniscule army and lots of oil. The fact that Kuwait was Iraq's erstwhile friend just made it less likely that they would expect a sneak attack.

Saddam's armed forces now poised in Iraq and Occupied Kuwait were equipped with MiG-29 fighters, which were comparable to the F-16 in capabilities and potential, Mirage F1s, which were bought from France and had shot down Iranian F-14s during the Iran-Iraq War, MiG-25s, which were extremely fast recon aircraft, Su-25s, which were excellent ground-attack planes, and finally the Scuds. Scuds are surface-to surface ballistic missiles only a few steps up from the old V-2 rocket that Hitler tried to use against London. This was the kind of missile used by both sides during the recent Iran-Iraq War but it wasn't very accurate... its optimal target was a city. It would be hard for it to miss a city. Smaller targets might be a problem.

To counter the threats posed by the "air breathers" and the ballistic missiles we had a lot of different weapons to do the same thing: shoot down an airplane. However, each weapon was designed to hit aircraft at different altitudes and different ranges and under different conditions. So, the Patriot could reach out and destroy enemy planes between 45-100 miles away (depending on what model Patriot missile it was equipped with), in a heavy electronic countermeasures environment and at high altitude, but could not see 360 degrees around. Hawk COULD see 360 degrees around and protect the Patriot systems. HAWK could also hit targets at ranges over 30 miles away and track low-altitude aircraft trying to come in under Patriot coverage. Chaparral was a tank –launched heat-seeking missile which could chase down an enemy aircraft out several miles but could be "spoofed" if the aircraft dropped flares or flew extremely low. Stinger was a shoulder-fire missile, more sophisticated, which didn't have the range of the Chaparral but would rapidly close on the target; it wouldn't be fooled by low-terrain unless the pilot was very lucky. And finally, Vulcan was a Gatling gun on a trailer or a tank. It served as the weapon of last resort, throwing up 1000 rounds per minute at close-range aircraft. And there was no fooling a Vulcan.

Patriot served a dual role: it could engage tactical ballistic missiles (TBMs) as well as conventional aircraft. In theory, anyway. It had intercepted some U.S.-made Lance missiles in tests a few years before but no one really knew how well it would work in combat conditions.

So the bottom line was that any aircraft attacking a U.S. Army unit would have to, ideally, fly through several layers of air defense coverage before getting the opportunity to drop bombs. In practice we worked with our own Air Force to make sure the enemy didn't get that close. And we kept a few surprises around, like the Alpha System, which served as a kind of an "Ace-in-the-Hole" for us hawkers, but was kept under wraps for a variety of reasons. While Saddam might have modified missiles and gas shells we had our own "secret weapon" hidden in plain sight...

STINGER GUNNERY PRACTICE

STINGER MISSILES WERE AN IMPORTANT PART OF OUR BATTERY'S ARSENAL AS THEY WERE SET UP IN AREAS THE HAWK COULDN'T "SEE."

What Saddam lacked in weapons of mass destruction he made up for in propaganda… and in some parts of the world (and on some campuses in the United States) it resonated with people. He tried to portray the struggle as a conflict between rich countries and poor ones. He offered free oil to any of these poor countries which attempted to break through the blockade which even then was strangling Iraq's economy.

No country was foolish enough to try it. Later Saddam tried to paint the war as one between the Zionists and the Anti-Zionists, which seems absurd when you consider how few Zionists must have been living in Kuwait in 1990. But he made noises about being victimized and how he was going to attack Israel "if a single bomb falls on Iraq," yada, yada, yada. Oh well. It DID give CNN something new to work into its 24-hour news cycle.

Saddam managed to get the support of Yemen and the PLO. This did not markedly change the strategic situation in his favor, as Yemen lacked a common border with Iraq and PLO lacked an ability to attack anything larger than a school bus of Israeli children.

There was a big briefing on September 22nd at Building 2. This was a presentation by several officers who had just returned from Saudi Arabia having been sent out in advance to serve as staff officers and to assess the needs of the growing international Coalition forming against Saddam.

Lieutenant Linker was one of the briefers. She had just spent 40 days as part of a USAF AWACS crew in the Gulf region. As an ADA officer, she explained how some of the first units in the country were Patriot batteries of 2-7 ADA. The Patriot systems were considered high-priority as the Air Force had conceded its inability to stop the threat posed by the scuds. They were initially reluctant to agree to other air defense systems being deployed to Saudi Arabia as the Air Force believed that it could establish Coalition air superiority, if not air supremacy.

This was an interesting viewpoint. In September 1990 it could be argued that the Coalition ONLY had "Air Parity," which means that it only controlled the skies over Coalition territory, i.e. Saudi Arabia. Now no one doubted that would change rapidly once actual hostilities began and that the Coalition air forces could gain control of airspace to the point where they could operate (in conjunction with land and sea forces) at times and places of their choice, i.e. "Air Superiority." However, the third and final level of air control, "Air Supremacy," means that you control the skies completely.

The last time I checked, tactical ballistic missiles travel through the skies, which made the normal definitions of air superiority and air supremacy moot.

Aside from the missile threat, according to Linker, the Air Force also had to concede that it was possible that the Iraqi Air Force could penetrate their fighter screen (especially if the IAF was willing to take a high number of casualties) and reach targets within Saudi Arabia. This would be bad under the best of circumstances... it would be catastrophic if some of those aircraft carried chemical weapons.

The Air Force was reluctant to use the Army's ground-based air defense systems to destroy these "leakers." Initially they told the ground force commanders that they would simply have to accept some level of risk. It was then explained to the Air Force that this would be the same level of risk assumed by the Coalition air bases. The Air Force withdrew its opposition and the 11th ADA Brigade would be deploying to both protect the Coalition ground forces... and the air bases.

"We're not going to be treated as step-children," concluded Linker. "In fact, everyone wants an air defense unit in their back yard."

Major Garner spoke next. He had just finished serving as a liaison officer to the Royal Saudi Air Defense Force. The Saudis had invested a lot of oil money into defense and some of that went into a variety of antiaircraft systems, including Hawk.

"Right now we are operating in a centralized mode, maintaining a direct link to the Air Force." said Garner. "They will assign us our targets."

This meant that we weren't to be used in the counter-air role, at least not right away. In this role the general in charge of all air operations (usually an Air Force general) designates a volume, or "box," called a Missile Engagement Zone. A MEZ can be almost any shape, with set upper and lower limits. It is prohibited for use by friendly aircraft which means that anything that enters it is hostile by default and can be shot down by the air defense missile systems defending it. This is an excellent tool for causing attrition among the enemy aircraft and for concentrating friendly aircraft elsewhere.

Command and control was currently directed by the Saudis. "This is a diagram showing the command and control structure," said Garner as he put up a vu-graph slide that looked as if it was dreamed up by someone in the Home for the Militarily Deranged. While we were all still trying to make sense of this incredibly complicated design someone behind me said in a loud voice "We're screwed." This met with understandable laughter.

"It's not as complicated as it appears," Garner said from the stage. "On a day-to-day basis it works."

He also spoke about the living conditions in the theater. "The Saudis are helping us out with food supplements, like fruit and such, and desalinized water. But for the time being it's going to be austere."

14

"It'll suck!" Someone said in a stage whisper, getting a few more laughs.

Major Garner told us how the Saudis were surprised at the speed in which the first Army units arrived on the ground. "They had no equipment available for the first units that arrived so 2-7 ended up borrowing space and equipment from the Air Force. My first night in-country I ended up sleeping less than 15 feet from an F-15. And the Patriot guys had to sleep in a TENT."

There was absolute silence until one of the SHORAD guys, the air defenders who actually live and operate with the Infantry, muttered "Those poor sons-of-bitches."

The whole place roared. You would have thought the USO had sent Robin Williams to entertain us.

Finally, after all the briefs and weeks of additional training it was time to go. Our household goods were turned in, our personally-owned cars were put in storage and the barracks were locked up. We were flying to Saudi Arabia to collect our equipment and get into the fight.

2. THE MAGIC KINGDOM

The first thing they gave us when we got off the plane was a plastic bottle of water. It helped. Getting off the L-1011 airliner we were hit by a wave of heat, like standing in front of an oven. Except that we would be *living* in this oven.

Welcome to Saudi Arabia.

We were given a second bottle of water and pretty soon were on our way to our billets at Cement City. One of the first things you learn about the Middle East is everything is a "city:" a construction site becomes Cement City, an amusement park is Entertainment City, a sports facility is Sport City and a factory zone is Industrial City. "Palace" was another term thrown around pretty loosely: Ice Palace, Gulf Palace and Blue Palace would all enter our frame of reference.

We drove through Dammam, near the port where we were expecting the ship loaded with our equipment. The drive through town was interesting, with signs in Arabic script. Some, like Coca-Cola and Kodak, were familiar enough to be recognized despite the language. There were several checkpoints manned by Saudis and Americans, and while there was some civilian traffic it was mostly military.

Whatever Cement City was before Desert Shield it was now home, however temporarily, to thousands of GIs. Warehouses provided shelter from the sun for lucky soldiers while others made do with large tents set up on either side of the main road. Home-made signs, mostly from MRE boxes, indicated who occupied the tent or had fun names like "Big Ben Bar and Grill," "The One-Hump Inn," "Pee Wee's Playhouse," Welcome to the Aviation Zone" and "The New Rick's Lounge." Or they had unimaginative names like "the Swamp." The whole facility had fencing and concrete barriers and concertina wire and MPs to keep out any bad guys who might have ideas about hitting us before we had a chance to get our equipment.

We were told to set up in an open area of one of the warehouses. Not long afterwards, as we started getting our cots and gear together we were told we had to move... the space was promised to someone else. After playing this game of Simon says (COLONEL Simon, apparently) we finally got settled in and were handed MREs, fresh bread and fruit.

Later on I was woken from a sound sleep. I had to turn in the personnel roster from the flight since I was the chalk commander. If I thought the paperwork was going to slack off just because war might break out at any minute I was badly mistaken.

Lt. Pace, who had been with the Advance Party, joined us and started filling us in on our home away from home. "The latrines are over by the fence line. Be careful when you use them: some of the units have been stealing the seats before they go over to their assembly areas."

"That's a bit inconsiderate, isn't it?" I absently asked as I looked through my MRE. No freeze-dried meat, thank goodness.

He pointed to the far end of the warehouse. "That's where the showers are. They have hours established for male and female use and you can only stay in for five minutes. They have MPs in the rafters to make sure everybody sticks to the limit."

"Yeah," piped in another one of the ADVON soldiers. "They start yelling at you pretty good if you stay in too long. Sometimes even if you haven't."

I looked at the long line of people waiting to get in and did some rapid calculations on my own personal funk factor versus inconvenience of use. "I don't think I'll need a shower that bad any time soon."

"What about news?" someone asked.

"News is pretty scarce out here. For some reason we don't get AFN. But you'll see some Stars and Stripes newspapers floating around, usually four or five days old. There are some unit newspapers, like the Desert Dragon, but they're not too good for information."

Pace then filled us in on Cement City's warning system. One siren blast meant "Accountability," and everyone was to assemble in their respective unit areas so commanders could make sure all soldiers, weapons and masks were accounted for. Two siren blasts meant "Stand-To"... all soldiers to grab their weapons and ammo and await further instructions. Three sirens meant "Gas:" all soldiers to go to MOPP[7] Level 4, which would result in each soldier putting on their protective pants and jacket, overboots, gloves, mask and hood. This was the best protection a soldier had against chemical attack. This was just another reminder that Saddam had his arsenal of chemical weapons standing by for use against us.

Jet lag and lack of sleep started kicking my butt after dark. I fell asleep early but woke up at 0300. It would take some time for my body to get used to the time difference. At 0600 we had our first formation "in-country:" all battery personnel lined up, everyone shouldering their M16 Automatic Rifle, everyone

---

[7] Mission-Oriented Protective Posture, for protection against chemical biological and nuclear weapons.

carrying their M17A1 Protective Mask on their left hip, everyone ready for action.

Except for that ONE person. One of the privates stood in formation without her mask and without her rifle. Apparently the magnitude of the moment had failed to impress her. She didn't think it was that big a deal. The battery First Sergeant vigorously set about changing her attitude and she soon ran back into the warehouse to go grab her gear.

First Sergeant Melanson was our "Top Sergeant," the senior NCO of the battery and the man in charge of accountability, Army standards and soldier care. The officers might make the decisions but the First Sergeant takes care of the soldiers and has a lot to do with how well orders are executed. We were lucky to have such a good NCO, although he had a few quirks of his own, such as a belief in astrology. Still, I would rather hear the First Sergeant talk about the influence Mars has on my destiny than listen to one of the BC's collection of bagpipe music tapes.

After formation it was time for chow. The mess hall was set up in a permanent building near the warehouses, but the line was 50 or 60 people long and breakfast was t-rats. T-rations were supposed to provide a simple but hot meal for troops in the field but these large metal containers (sealed for storage, opened with a can opener) were usually pretty bad. I settled for an orange instead.

Back in the warehouse someone else had decided we were in the wrong spot and once again cots and gear were being moved to another part of the warehouse. I somehow managed to get to sleep.

I was awakened not long afterwards by Captain Fletcher. "James, I need you to take a detail of twenty people to the port of Dhahran. We need our people over there to help with the ships when they arrive."

So I somehow managed to get moving, get dressed, get the detail together and get my gear and my rifle and be ready to get on the bus. Two busses actually pulled up in front of the warehouse and it took some work to squeeze my 20 people on them but we made it. Our Saudi drivers then proceeded to scare the hell out of us, executing lane changes at random and blasting their horns at intervals to inform other drivers he they were about to do something crazy. If there are traffic laws in Saudi Arabia they didn't seem to be enforced... except of course that one about no women drivers. The road signs and traffic systems seem to be European for the most part.

PHONING HOME FROM THE MAGIC KINGDOM

Most of the buildings we passed were new and modern, although a few had an Islamic "twist." A lot of the autos speeding along were of recent make too. It only seemed as if the people, walking about wearing the same outfits their great-great-great-great-great-grandparents would have worn, were the ones who were out of place.

We arrived at Warehouse 20 at the Dhahran docks. Or at least SOME of us arrived. We soon noticed that the other bus had completely disappeared. It would be three hours before it rolled in after getting lost in traffic. One soldier muttered as he climbed out "the roads here are so confusing that even the Saudis don't know where they're going."

Warehouse 20 would be our home for the next several days. I had a formation and got 100% accountability (they taught us to do that sort of thing at ROTC Advanced Camp) and met up with a staff NCO from the Imperial Brigade. I was told that we were here to work as part of a brigade detail to unload all air defense artillery equipment from our ship, which was expected sometime in the next few days. The whole time we were at the docks I could never figure out what the problem was with at least telling us what DAY the ship would arrive. I mean, was the ship on radio silence in order to evade Saddam's u-boats? Was it waiting to broadcast its position until after it broke through the Iraqi blockade? There was probably a good reason for the confusion but it was never made obvious to me.

We made ourselves about as comfortable as circumstances would permit, what with heavy artillery and other machines rolling down one side of the building and big ships unloading on the other. I let the soldiers get sleep and relax. I know I needed to get over jet lag.

Some of the soldiers tried fishing, but the only thing available for bait was the contents from the MREs and the fish didn't seem that keen for freeze-dried pork patties. A couple guys tried to catch fish in a hammock. One guy explained to the other that what they needed to do was throw one end of the net into the water while the other hung on to his end. They stood on the dock, each one holding one side of the hammock. "On three... ONE... TWO... THREE!" and they both threw their ends out into the water. As the net sank into the Persian Gulf they argued with each other about who was supposed to hang on and who was supposed to throw. Chinese seamen from the freighter docked at the pier laughed their butts off.

Our routine was one of establishing accountability for everyone, their weapon and their protective mask, eating (either at the mess trailer set up by 5-62 ADA or by collecting MREs) and entertaining ourselves as best we could.

Frisbee, football, fishing (at least until some sergeant-major came along and said it was *verboten*[8] from the docks), cooking out, sitting on the breakers at "China Beach," listening to "boom boxes," playing cards and reading, and reading, and reading. There wasn't much in the way of water sports

Periodically the Call to Prayer would play on the speaker systems of nearby mosques. Big cranes moved around the area and lots of vehicles traveled the docks. Saudi gun trucks, which were very light Toyota pickup trucks armed with heavy machine guns, drove around the dock areas but I know I for one wondered if the trucks wouldn't get bowled over by the recoil if they tried hitting something on either side of the truck. The gun trucks weren't military models by any stretch of the imagination and even still had glossy paint jobs.

One frustration for me was the lack of communication between us and the bulk of our unit back at Cement City. I had no phone number, no radio system, not even a vehicle in which I could send a courier back in. Another aggravation came when we had to move ourselves and our gear to another part of Warehouse 20 because we were occupying the "wrong area." It seemed like ever since we arrived in Saudi Arabia we were just like Madonna: sleeping in a different spot every night.

No one could tell us when our ship would arrive... until it suddenly showed up on October 23rd! Suddenly it was all panic as the NCO placed in charge of the unloading started collecting the first shift of soldiers and putting them in duty uniform. We got them fed and put them on transport for the dock where the ship waited three miles away. I was designated the S1 (personnel officer) for this operation which meant keeping track of where all our people were.

Soon after the troops were sent to the ship a tactical truck arrived back at the dock, driven by Staff Sergeant Harmon of my battery. "Ready to go over to the ship, Sir?"

I grabbed a baloney sandwich and a Pepsi and jumped in. I noticed the unit markings as I ran up. "Hey, doesn't this belong to 5-62?"

Harmon shrugged. "They haven't got any of ours out yet. Besides, 5-62 doesn't need it right now."

We passed through the warehouse checkpoint and Harmon, almost as an afterthought, said "You know, the 5-62 guys would really be pissed if they knew we had one of their trucks." Now it was MY turn to shrug.

---

[8] In those days a tour of duty in West Germany was a normal part of an Army career, as that was where WWIII was expected. Everyone seemed to pick up at least a LITTLE German.

MREs WERE NOT AS BAD AS ALL
THAT BUT STILL NOT AS GOOD AS
C-RATS HAD BEEN. THE MAIN
ADVANTAGE THEY HAD WAS THAT
THE MRE IS LIGHTER.

And wouldn't you know it, the first person we run into at the unloading operation was a First Sergeant from the 5th Battalion, 62nd Air Defense Artillery. And he was indeed pissed.

"Where the Hell do you guys get off, taking one of our trucks?!" he demanded. He went on to use some rather descriptive terms for the two of us, and while I mentally noticed that the word "Sir" was never added to the phrases and combinations he was using we WERE in the wrong and it seemed as if the smartest thing we could do was give up the machine with as much dignity as we could muster and try to redeem ourselves in work.

The USNS Algol was being unloaded at the dock. A fast sealift vessel, it had a side ramp so vehicles could drive on and off and vehicles from the brigade were being driven off. I went aboard and was amazed at how much open space there was in the ship's A and B decks. Unfortunately, in the loading at Beaumont, Texas, maximized space but cut a couple of corners. Sheared retention pins, broken towing pintles, scratches, dents and the complete crushing of one of my battery's IFF antenna housings formed part of the tally but once cooler heads assessed the damage there turned out to be little that could not be replaced or repaired.

Harder to deal with would be electronic problems stemming from cable shearing and loose components. We would spend considerable time running down the odd problem resulting from the 1990 sea cruise.

Morale was high, since this was the real thing and not just another exercise. When there was poor morale it was due to poor management of the soldiers... such as making them move from one spot in a warehouse to another.

October 25th. Just as work crews were leaving the warehouse for the Algol the air raid sirens sounded from the towers located around the docks. No one did anything. No one knew if it was a drill or if a scud was on its way or if an Iraqi Air Force suicide squad was on its way, but not a single person reacted because no one else did.

My skin crawled. I HATE air raid sirens.

Everyone breathed a sigh of relief when the sirens wound down after a couple of minutes. We began going about our business, chalking up the air raid warning to a monthly test, when the sirens started up again. Not all the sweating was due to the heat now.

SFC Makaloney came by and informed us that the sirens were indeed part of a test. He had been informed of the impending test earlier that morning but somehow that info never got shared.

After 45 minutes of nerve-wracking noise the sirens finally wound down and a voice went out over the sound system: "test complete."

Gracious living at Dharhan. We were stuck in a warehouse while we waited for our ship with the Hawk system to arrive.

The view outside the warehouse. Like everything else it was "hurry up and wait..." until the ship showed up. then things got crazy really fast.

We were all shaking off the effects of the sirens when they kicked on again! My nerves were getting frazzled. The sheer stupidity of such tests would encourage complacency until REAL missiles started flying over the borders.

Back at the ship things weren't going well. In order to get the towed equipment off the ship as quickly as possible vehicles with towing pintles were being grabbed willy-nilly and were taking radars, missile launchers and generators off regardless of whether they were the ideal vehicle for towing that particular piece of equipment. Worse, the equipment was getting mixed up at the holding area and just sorting it out promised to be a major job.

Never having even discussed the possibility of sealift operations before this[9] our soldiers were just overwhelmed. We finished unloading the Algol at 1800 and congratulated ourselves on a job well-done. We ate and some of the soldiers crashed out. THEN we were told that there was a deck we missed on the Algol and it still had 18 of our vehicles.

"How do you miss an entire deck?!" I asked SFC Harmon.

"I don't know, Sir." He answered tiredly. "All I know is that we have to get them off."

So now we have to scare up two details to finish the job. Needless to say, none of the soldiers were happy about being "voluntold" for more work. It was a long night but we got the remaining deck cleared.

Back at the warehouse I crashed out on my cot, dead-tired.

The next morning the real fun began. The equipment had to be moved from the holding area to a gravel lot where it would be sorted by unit (and, of course, individual weapon systems). The lot was too small to set each firing platoon up in full operational mode but was large enough to check out individual pieces of equipment and to do connectivity checks. Meanwhile, one of the Patriot batteries was set up in another lot nearby in full readiness in case of air or missile attack.

Bravo Battery was the first to collect all its equipment and get set up. The long process of checking out every circuit, every component for faults was supervised by the warrant officers. Meanwhile, we were down four soldiers: one with a swollen hand and another with a swollen foot (possibly due to an allergic reaction to insect bites) and two others with dysentery. One of them was Lieutenant Pace and his condition was so serious that there was talk of him being shipped out of the theater for medical treatment.

---

[9] If WWIII broke out we were supposed to get airlifted to Europe.

HOW
HAWK
WORKS

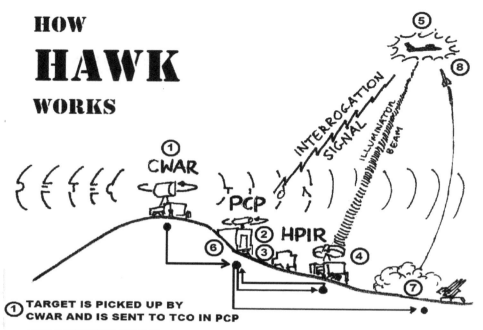

1. **TARGET IS PICKED UP BY CWAR AND IS SENT TO TCO IN PCP**

2. **TCO SENDS IFF SIGNAL TO DETERMINE IF TARGET IS FRIENDLY OR HOSTILE**

3. **UPON NEGATIVE IFF SIGNAL THE TCO "ORDERS" LOCK-ON WITH HIPIR**

4. **HIPIR "AIMS" BEAM AT TARGET USING INFORMATION RECEIVED FROM CWAR AND RO**

5. **TARGET IS "ILLUMINATED" WITH ENERGY THAT THE HAWK MISSILE WILL "SEE"**

6. **TCO PUSHES "FIRE" BUTTON**

7. **LAUNCHER "AIMS" AT TARGET AND FIRES MISSILE**

8. **MISSILE "HOMES IN" ON HIPIR ENERGY AND DESTROYS TARGET**

BY DESERT STORM HAWK MISSILE SYSTEMS WERE VERY STREAMLINED AND FAIRLY MOBILE

Captain Fletcher gathered his remaining LTs and the senior NCOs together to give them their tasks. Our priority was to get the weapon systems up and running and to be prepared to move out to field positions where we could defend the tactical units (infantry, armor and artillery) moving out to the desert to stop Saddam if he chose to cross the border into Saudi Arabia. There was one road which led from Baghdad to Kuwait City to Dammam... right where we were! As part of the bigger effort we would be part of the blocking force for any further Iraqi movements.

But first we had to get the weapon systems operational. Officially, we operated HAWK III, the third-generation of an air defense system that the Army had been using since the 1950s. This system had evolved since first fielded until it reached the configuration we used. Each battery was divided into two fire platoons, which operated miles apart and ideally were mutually supporting. Each platoon consisted of a Continuous Wave Acquisition Radar (CWAR), a High-Power Illuminator Radar (HPIR[10], or just "High-Power"), a Platoon Command Post (PCP), a Junction Box (J-Box) and variety of generators, communication systems and three launchers each carrying three missiles. There was also the Pulse Acquisition Radar (PAR) but more on that in a moment.

To shoot down an aircraft the CWAR would detect it first, sending radar waves well beyond the range of the missiles. Once detected by the CWAR it would appear on the radar scope in the PCP, where the Tactical Control Officer (a lieutenant) would see it and decide what to do about it. An antenna on the roof of the PCP would send an IFF signal to determine if the aircraft was friendly or not. If it was NOT and it was in range and other tactical considerations were met then the LT could "lock on" using the HIPIR. This sent a very intense radar beam to the target which lit it up in energy invisible to humans but bright as a neon light to a Hawk missile's seeker system. The radar operator for the HIPIR sat to the TCO's left. Once a good lock was established the lieutenant (that's me!) pushed the fire button, sending at least one of our airborne killers to the fighter or transport or helicopter or whoever it was whose number was up.

That is, this is how it worked under ideal conditions. Under conditions in which you are dealing with an enemy pilot who KNOWS you are there (he has detected your radars) and does NOT want to be shot down, there are things like electronic countermeasures and certain maneuvers which will make it hard to hit him. One item out of our bag of tricks is to track the target visually without the radar, using a video camera installed in between the antennas of the HIPIR.

---

[10] We'll use the acronym "HIPIR" which more approximated the normal pronunciation of the name. We will not include some of the more common adjectives used with the name, however.

The RO's scope becomes a television screen and he keeps the target in the cross-hairs until the moment is ideal and then... the HIPIR is turned back on again and is already aimed directly at the target. A push of the fire button and at that range the pilot has a missile in the cockpit with him before he has a chance to figure out what that "Launch Detected" alarm is all about.

Another tactic the enemy might use is attack for the express purpose of taking out our missile site altogether. This type of mission is known as a Wild Weasel. The enemy aircraft maneuvers close enough to fire an Anti-Radiation Missile, or ARM, which homes in and destroys radars. Most of the ARMs we were used to dealing with were easy to spoof... you turned off the radar. No radar, nothing to home in one... the missile presumably flies past and crashes somewhere else, harmlessly you hope. But it turned out that Saddam had got some very new model ARMs from the Soviets... these "remembered" your location even if you turned off the radar.

So our solution to this new ARM threat was actually pretty clever. We used the PAR, a leftover from the original HAWK I system.[11] It was a long-range radar system, which allowed us to see targets at a great distance, much farther than they could be engaged. However, when integrated into the Net we could watch radar returns from AWACS, other Hawk fire units, Patriot, etc. and the PAR was rarely used anymore. The radar was in fact universally disliked because its signal was so powerful that it easily gave away our location to any enemy who knew what to listen for... even in a neighboring country.

But thanks to some new software the PAR could now "see" an inbound ARM and identify it at long range. However, you had to know what the signature looked like and you had to fire on it immediately... you would only get one chance to shoot down the ARM.

Yet another tactic, and one that didn't rely on new technology, might be to overwhelm us with sheer numbers of aircraft. In normal mode you can't defeat a swarm by calmly engaging each enemy plane one at a time. Even spending just a few seconds on each target would add up as more and more aircraft got close enough to use their weapons.

Under these circumstances there was always LASHE mode. Instead of a searchlight beam the HIPAR would send out a fan... and every target in the fan would be illuminated for an individual missile which would be rapidly launched one after another until all nine missiles were gone. Very impressive but if there are more than nine airplanes flying at you then you had better hope that the

---

[11] Other Hawk dinosaurs include the Range-Only-Radar (ROR) and the Battery Command Central (BCC). The only thing that distinguished the PAR from the ROR and the BCC was that the PAR wasn't quite extinct yet.

HIDING IN THE DESERT

survivors are utterly demoralized... there would be little you could do until those launchers were reloaded, one at a time.

Some electronic countermeasures were designed to blind or confuse the system. We would respond to ECM with electronic counter-counter-measures. They, of course, would respond with electronic-counter-counter-counter-measures and this could keep up until either the enemy plane runs out of fuel or the radar operator makes a mistake and forgets whose turn it is.

The enemy might try to sneak into blind spots in the radar coverage. This would not work out well for him either. The TCO can "see" radar returns from many other detections systems, including other Hawk units, long-range surveillance radars, even Patriot (although we failed to get that capability to work back at Fort Bliss). Plus we had Stinger teams set up in spots where the enemy might try to fly under the radar... at perfect altitude for the teams.

And on top of all that we had the Alpha System. The additional equipment to operate it was installed in the PCP and the disguised sensor system had arrived intact. We would be operating it in a combat environment for the first time, but first we had to get the main system working.

Hawk had seen service in several of the Israeli-Arab wars. It had been part of NATO's air defense network for decades. It had guarded Florida's shores for a time after the Cuban Missile crisis. It had even been employed by the Kuwaitis to destroy an airborne invasion of Kuwait City just a few months ago.[12]

So why couldn't we get ours to work?

There I was, sitting in the PCP staring at the screen on the TDECC, or control panel, wearing my headset to communicate to the Tactical Director, whose job was to watch all the battalion's Hawk returns and to pick and choose targets as necessary. The TD also monitored the readiness of each fire platoon and gave instructions to maximize coverage.

I had to sit on a J-Box. We hadn't managed to find the chairs for the van yet.

"Bravo One[13]?" I heard on the headset.

I responded to the platoon's call sign. "This is Bravo-One."

---

[12] Kuwait's Hawk batteries supposedly prevented the capture of the Emir's family by airborne units during the August invasion. The Iraqi ground offensive later captured several batteries of equipment. It was doubtful that the Iraqis could get the system functioning or keep it running without outside technical help.

[13] There are some contradictions in my post-DS notes about our call signs. I believe the call signs may have changed at one or more points during the operation. For clarity's sake I have used the same call signs throughout.

"Roger, I'm going to send you a pointer."

I watched the screen. Nothing new or interested happened there.

After about a minute I heard "Bravo-One?"

"This is Bravo-One. I've got nothing on my screen."

"Roger, we will continue to work on it from our end."

It was frustrating. We had inspected each individual piece of equipment, had done a few minor repairs necessitated by the sea cruise, got each piece to talk to each other... but we still could not integrate with the battalion via the datalink. Plus I had an IFF Fail and a HIPIR Fail indicated on the status display. The HIPIR turned out to be caused by a bent plug but the IFF problem persisted.

Staff Sergeant Lynn and Chief Dungy took a look at it. They referred the IFF problem to 34th Ordnance, our battalion maintenance company. A Hawk mechanic from the 34th referred it over to an electronic specialist and soon there were five people crammed into the PCP's limited working space, all of them poking at the IFF controls.

Meanwhile, someone decided to take apart the ADP, the central computer for the system, and see if that would help with the integration problem. By now the 2nd Platoon was fully functional. But looking at the guts of the ADP didn't help 1st Platoon get operational.

Finally, someone thought to look at the programmed data. And there it was: a data-entry error on our position which mistakenly put us a thousand miles north of our position. A couple of wrong numbers were all it took to not just leave us "inop" but to also soak up a lot of resources needed elsewhere in the battalion.

The IFF was fixed later on that same day. Both of our battery's fire platoons were fully operational. I celebrated by taking a shower and lying down on my cot with a book I bought before I left the States.

3. RADAR HILL

November 1st. My day started at 0350. I got dressed and grabbed my stuff. We were off to find our first two operational Hawk sites in Saudi Arabia.

Each fire platoon had an RSOP Team, a Reconnaissance, Selection and Occupation of Position element. The small team (let by a junior lieutenant) moved to where the fire platoon was going to operate next, located the best position for it (preferably with high terrain) and laid out the positions for each individual piece of equipment. The site would then be secured until the rest of the unit arrived.

Like so many other things this move would not be according to the book: normally one platoon stays and provides air defense coverage while the other platoon moves[14]. In this case both platoons would be moving out together until they reached the vicinity of the two future missile sites.

We had a trusty Saudi guide to show us where to go. We also had two heavy transporters with us carrying a scooploader (in case we had to do some light engineering), showers and portable latrines. The civilian drivers had operated their transporters for Saddam only a couple of years before, helping to move his tanks from one place to another on the battle front during the Iran-Iraq War.

I guess a job is a job.

I walked down the line, talking to each driver, asking them if their vehicle checked out. Each one confirmed that their machine was road-ready. I looked at the towing pintels for each piece of equipment we were taking with us and checked the tail light hookups, brake lines, etc. I climbed into my own B103, a CUCV[15], or "Blazer." Finally, we were ready to go. We headed north into the desert.

I've been in deserts before but this one was simply empty: no palm trees, no camels, no buildings, but overpasses every few miles. Roads to nowhere.

---

[14] Air defense units on the road are extremely vulnerable to (what else?) air attack.

[15] A Commercial Utility Cargo Vehicle, this was basically a replacement for the jeep until HMMWVs became widely available. The Army was willing to pay good money for what was basically a badly-engineered civilian off-road station wagon instead of, oh, I don't know... civilian jeeps? CUCVs were notable for almost always having the rear window smashed out due to a design flaw.

32

One of the Stinger humvees sat a rest stop on the way to our first missile sites. The Stingers are kept in the green "coffins" in the back and provided air defense of the RSOP team if it became necessary.

A hazard of the desert: sinking into the sand. This was B103, an Army Blazer and the RSOP "scout vehicle." Note the battery logo stenciled on the door: a palm tree with an ADA emblem.

Lieutenant Phil Riley was riding up front with the Saudi. The little guy spoke at least some English and was friendly enough. He talked to Phil about the fact that his father was a general and that he would have to salute and ask permission from him in order to see his mother.

He was interested in America and Americans. He also asked Phil how he got so big.

"I eat all kinds of stuff, meat and potatoes, stuff like that."

The Saudi paused for a moment. "Ham?"

"Oh yeah," Phil smiled. "I LIKE ham!"

The Saudi made a disgusted face and drove on.

Things were going, if not well then at least predictably, given the state of our Vietnam-era trucks and the stop-gap replacement for the jeep, the CUCVs. One generator tire blew and a CUCV had to be coaxed back on the road but we were still moving. We made it to a Saudi truck stop, a kind of roadway oasis.

That was when we found out that one of the trucks was on "empty." The driver, a sergeant, had failed to check his fuel level. Apparently when I asked whether the truck was ready he misunderstood me to mean "is everything OK with your truck... OTHER than fuel?"

We had no fuel truck with us nor any jerry cans. We were discussing how to siphon fuel and if we could balance the consumption to get all vehicles to the sites when one of the enlisted soldiers said "This is a gas station... why don't we just BUY some diesel?"

And that's what we ended up doing. We dreaded the cost of actually shelling out cash for the fuel but it came to a whopping $4.00. It turned out that in oil-rich Saudi Arabia diesel was dirt-cheap and Phil gladly paid it.

That was the good news. The bad news was that Lieutenant Riley was stuck with that particular sergeant and that would turn out to be a major problem later. Riley was a good officer, a great TCO and he had an excellent sense of humor. But things like a driver neglecting to check his fuel before a convoy was enough to try even HIS patience.

As our small convoy pulled out a Saudi family with what must have been all their family possessions loaded on a truck cheered at us. They appeared to be going south as we went north. Sergeant Young, my driver, laughed. "They're saying 'go get 'em!'"

Two more vehicle breakdowns on the way: one involving a fuel pump and the other with a brake problem. The wrecker starter towing the truck with the busted fuel pump but we pulled over to work on the machine with the bad brakes. A U.S. field artillery unit rolled past and headed off into the desert, obviously on its way to set up a firebase. We were now in the 24th Mech.

The RSOP convoy, pulled up at the base of what would become Radar Hill. Missing was the wrecker and an additional truck, which would make it later.

Sgt. Young (left) and Lt. Whitmire doing their daily hygiene near Radar Hill. At this point we were waiting for the rest of the battery to arrive from Dhahran. Radar equipment and launchers already had their positions staked out, as well as the "admin area" locations.

Division's assembly area and couldn't help but to notice how the artillery unit was equipped with brand-new HEMMTs and HUMMVs. "Meanwhile, we're stuck with Vietnam surplus..." muttered Young.

We made it to the area were supposed to set up in but by now the wrecker was overheating: the strain of pulling another truck in the heat was too much for it. We left it and the truck it was towing on the paved road, designated Main Supply Route Mercedes by the Army. We then proceeded to locate good missile sites for the battery, one on either side of the road.

We found a great location for AFP 1, the main fire platoon and the one in which all the battery support would be located. It was a very large hill and high enough to dominate the surrounding desert, giving the acquisition radar a very long "reach." It also had level escarpments, ideal for setting up the other pieces of equipment needed to track and destroy targets.

We established true north and the site grid coordinates and used the M2 Aiming Circle to "shoot" each piece of equipment from a central location. Signs were set up showing where each piece of equipment would be set up when it arrived. Meanwhile, a commo team set up some of the radios and the first antennas went up on what would become nicknamed "Radar Hill." Miles away, Lieutenant Riley did the same for his site to the East, but he ran into a few problems.

Apparently some Armor colonel belonging to the 24th Mechanized Infantry Division had spotted the hill that the 2nd platoon was going to use for their Hawk missile system. He pulled up as the RSOP team was laying out the location and asked "What the Hell are you doing on my land?!"

The team tried to explain why the high ground was so important for the Hawk system but this colonel was having none of it... he was dead-set on using that hill to park his tanks. WHY it was important to have the tanks on high ground was beyond me, but certainly the 24th Mech would have been better served by having a surface-to-air missile set up with max coverage overhead. Instead, AFP2 had to move to a less-than-optimum site.

Because Patriot and Hawk units were rarely seen by folks at levels lower than corps, we were not as appreciated as we should have been. During the delay of the arrival of the rest of the Hawk equipment I rode in the Blazer to the 24th Mech's headquarters area to get some potable (i.e., drinkable) water. I knew we were in the right place because it was set up on a big hill (NOT the one AFP2 had been on) surrounded by rows of concertina wire, bunkers and even a Vulcan doing double duty as antiaircraft gun and ground defense weapon.

"I.D." the guard demanded. I passed my card over to Young who gave it to the soldier.

"Unit?" he asked, eyeballing me.

"Bravo Battery, 2ⁿᵈ Battalion. 1ˢᵗ ADA." I replied.

In a polite but almost condescending way he asked "Are you sure you're in the right place, Sir? This IS the 24ᵗʰ Mech." The implication being of course that we must be either lost or rear-echelon sight-seeing the area where the action was going to be.

"My battery is covering your ass." I answered. "Look, all we're here for is water."

"To the left, Sir." And he waved us through.

So we found ourselves "orphans" in the Army scheme of things. While we provided the invisible "umbrella" which protected the troops on the ground those same troops saw no reason why they should provide any sort of support to us, whether it was PX access, replacement parts or phone centers for "morale calls." This wasn't so much the fault of the senior officers, as I assume they understood our role and why we were there, but more that of the NCOs and officers at the lower end who suffered from "patch prejudice."

On the way back we got stuck within a few hundred yard of Radar Hill. Still no sign of the rest of the battery. I sent a soldier who was riding in the vehicle up ahead to see if we could get a truck to tow us out.

Sergeant Young and I sat in the vehicle, looking at the hill. Suddenly I spotted something. "Hey, isn't that the scooploader?"

Young leaned forward a little. "Where?"

"Up there, on the hill."

He just squinted.

"WITH ALL THE WHEELS UP!"

"Holy…!" Young stirred himself and jumped out of the Blazer. We both stared up near the peak of the hill where the scooploader, which we used as bulldozer, crane and forklift, was resting on its cab with its tires pointed upward in a hole it had seemingly dug for itself.

When a truck came down to get us we found out that the scooploader had overturned while digging out the site. The operator, Specialist James Brown, was OK… although the generator mechanic told us that the scooploader was NOT OK.

And sure enough, Specialist Brown was sitting on top of the machine[16] smoking a cigarette when we got up there. Despite rolling the entire scooploader he didn't have a scratch on him. He was lucky… that time.

It turned out that a tire blew while it was clearing part of the hill. The cab was not crushed but it seemed like a miracle that Brown wasn't killed. He was a good mechanic and an asset to us and without him it would have been

---

[16] Or what USED to be the bottom.

OPERATIONAL IN
SAUDI ARABIA

even harder to keep our old trucks running. Being a skilled operator on some of our heavy equipment made him that much more important to us.

About 1300 the rest of the battery arrived. Everything ran like clockwork: each vehicle towing a piece of the Hawk system was met and guided into position on the hill. Once in their positions the crewmembers for that piece began the process of leveling, stabilizing, energizing and integrating each piece of equipment into the fire platoon system. Unfortunately the CWAR and the PAR would not come online at the same time. And the ground was hard as a rock in certain areas, making it difficult to put in grounding rods. And on top of all this, the generators kept threatening to give out. But somehow we got everything running.

The wrecker arrived at the site of the accident. Somehow, our mechanics were able to get that scooploader out of a really awkward spot, but it took a couple of hours. They then proceeded to work on defensive emplacements around the missile site and clear areas and to make simple roads to reach everything.

Meantime, the system was integrated internally but not allowed to radiate, or send out radar waves. This was so the system could escape detection by the Iraqis, who had Il-76 jet transports retrofitted with special equipment which might or might not be able to detect electronic emissions and send that info to "wild weasels"... fighter bombers trained and equipped to wipe out enemy radars.

In parallel with conventional HAWK system we emplaced and activated our secret weapon system, the IIIA. Well, it was secret and it was a weapon, anyway. It was the Alpha System.

Hawk had gone through three generations, or models, over the years. These were known as Phase I, Phase II and the newest one was Phase III. These involved reconfiguring how the system worked in combat, improved radars, etc. But our unit was equipped with Phase IIIA. And this system had a surprise built in.

As I learned during my late night visits to a non-descript warehouse at Fort Bliss,[17] IIIA included the basic Phase III system with key add-ons which would actually give it two different types of missiles with which to engage the enemy: the standard missile, which usually homed in on a target illuminated by the HIPIR, and the Alpha missile,[18] which looked identical to the standard but in

---

[17] The only school in which my drawings were classified "SECRET" and which I had to sign an SF312 Classified Information Non-Disclosure Agreement

[18] MIM-23X? I have no idea what the official designation for this missile was but it appeared to be identical to a 23-series missile.

fact homed in on various electronic emissions given off by the target's avionics: on-board warning radar, navigation radio, that sort of thing.

The two missile systems operated separately from each other, only sharing power from the battery's generators. The Alpha system was passive, as opposed to Hawk's active radar which continually sent out signals. It was this passive nature which made it impossible to detect until launch.

A target would first be picked up by the Sensor, which was disguised as a standard 60kw generator. There were several of these powering the system so an additional one wouldn't be noticed. This information would then be fed to a readout on an "add-on" to the Platoon Command Post's control panel. It would provide an azimuth reading of potential targets and the model aircraft it was. The identification was made based on a profile of the aircraft's avionics, so instead of being told a plane was "friendly," hostile" or "unknown" based on a coded ID signal response (or lack thereof) this system could tell a MiG-25 from an F-15 without ever sending out a signal and giving its position away. In theory, anyway.

The reason for the secrecy was that if an enemy KNEW you were using his avionics against him in this way he could turn some of them off (screwing up the Alpha's ability to identify the aircraft's make) or even turn off ALL of them, rendering the aircraft "invisible" to it (but not to a fully operational Hawk system, which would still track and fire on targets using radar). But ideally, the TCO could fire on a target in stealth mode from the single Alpha-equipped launcher once the launch command was given. With any luck, an Alpha missile could slam into an enemy plane while the pilot was still waiting for a radar warning light to come on.

But because of the weakness in the weapon's operating principle, secrecy was as much a part of the Alpha system as the sensor or the missiles. Without secrecy the system was useless. As a result, very few people in the battery even knew we actually operated two different weapon systems.

Both systems worked independently of each other but were operated by the TCO. If one system was damaged the other could still shoot down airplanes. The system was simple to operate and the course was short. But only the LTs were trained on the system so we were on our own when it came to getting everything on the Alpha System running, including the fake generator.

Alpha worked well in simulation but how it would work in combat was anybody's guess.

It was dark as most of the soldiers worked on getting the administrative and living areas established and the downrange crew loaded the missiles onto the launchers. Once the last missile was in place we were ready to fight.

HOW
ALPHA
WORKS

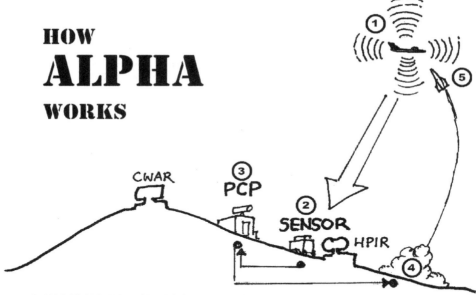

1. POTENTIAL TARGET PROVIDES FOUR TYPES OF AVIONIC EMISSIONS

2. ALPHA SENSOR, CLEVERLY DISGUISED AS A GENERATOR, DETECTS EMISSIONS AND SENDS DATA TO PCP

3. COMPUTER PROVIDES SPECIFIC AIRFRAME ID BASED ON LIBRARY, LISTS TARGETS BASED ON THEIR SIGNAL STRENGTH

4. SPECIAL LAUNCHER IS GIVEN LAUNCH COMMAND BY TCO; AIMS IN GENERAL DIRECTION OF TARGET

5. ALPHA MISSILE, OUTWARDLY IDENTICAL TO HAWK MISSILE, HOMES IN SIGNAL MATCH GIVEN BY ALPHA SENSOR

THE ALPHA PROMISED A BUILT-IN IDENTIFICATION SYSTEM BASED ON WHAT EMISSIONS THE AIRCRAFT PRODUCED.

We began to get into a routine. We integrated with other batteries electronically, sharing air picture data. We received a schedule as to when we could radiate and different batteries took turns providing area radar coverage. When an Iraqi "al-AWACS" got airborne we would get a message to shut down radars to prevent them from getting a fix. Meantime, we would perform our daily maintenance and operational checks at the battery level, keep an eye on the airspace and maintain our DA1594 Daily Staff Journal Or Officer's Log. Crew shifts were usually four on, eight off.

Individual fire units were controlled by a Tactical Director, or TD, located at a control van (ICC) at battalion headquarters. The TD's job was to prevent missile wastage by allocating specific targets to each system, to provide early warning of inbound hostiles, and to prevent fratricide. The TD would control the air battle (or our part of it, at least) by setting parameters during which we could or could not engage.

So now we waited, providing an invisible "shield" over our troops in eastern Saudi Arabia. The Iraqis didn't seem eager to challenge the Coalition that was building up in the desert but Saddam had already proven himself a wildcard and he did have a reputation for using chemical weapons. Our missiles were kept "off line" for safety reasons but could be brought under control of the TCO at the flip of a switch if or when the shooting started.

While the weapon system was doing its job and being tested and maintained the rest of the sections had their tasks as well. Our Stinger missile teams were sent out to areas identified as possible "blank spots," areas too low for effective radar coverage. These two-man teams would hit any plane trying to fly under our radar coverage with their shoulder-fired antiaircraft missile. The Stinger didn't carry anything near the punch of a Hawk, but there was a good chance it would actually strike the target[19], causing maximum damage. At night, when the Stinger was ineffective, the teams drove back to their parent sites.

The Stinger crews would also use their brand-new HUMMV's to go on special runs and the crews helped out with the ground defenses of the main site. They took pride in their nickname: "Air Defense Infantry."

The Admin Section, run by Staff Sergeant Lacher, tracked fuel consumption, our water supply, the mail, and everything else that made life in the desert possible. He was responsible for communications as well and the tactical radio and phones were linked through the Battery Command Post.

We had a public announcement system rigged up to inform the site of alerts and other important info. We managed to rig the system up to play music

---

[19] This is called a "contact kill." Most air defense weapons rely on a proximity fuze of some kind in order to detonate in the vicinity of the target, relying on shrapnel to cause critical damage.

as well, but this was only done on special occasions or on "off" days, like Sunday, when our Soldiers had an opportunity to relax a bit.

Almost every soldier had their own music, thanks to walkmans, boom boxes and even a handful of CD players. Music available at our site ranged from classical to rap to country-and-western. Some of our soldiers brought entire tape collections. Later, Armed Forces Radio would broadcast to Coalition soldiers throughout the region.

Vehicle maintenance was carried out on a daily basis, as per the book. Staff Sergeant Harmon usually had at least one truck being repaired by the mechanics on any given day (not surprising, given the number of "road failures" we had in getting to our operational site) while his parts clerk Specialist Williams had her hands full just trying to get the bits and pieces we needed to keep the machines running. One item which was particularly hard to get seemed to be tires. A lot were being sent to the U.S. Army from European and American companies but few of them reached us.

The 34th Ordnance Company, our battalion-level maintenance asset, could do vehicle repairs that our mechanics couldn't handle at the battery level. The 34th Ord. could take a while though, spending days or weeks on a repair. Later we found out that a nearby Florida National Guard Ordnance Brigade could do the work for us, and they gladly replaced a couple of our truck engines.

The Motors Section also fueled up the generators. The generator mechanics had their hands full keeping the electricity going without trying to refuel the things as well. If anything the generators were in worse shape than the trucks.

The Mess Section fixed two hot meals a day: breakfast and dinner. The section had its own mess trailer for preparing and serving meals but it wasn't until later that we received a colorful Arab tent to eat it in. Naturally we called the dining tent the Big Top, and it was relatively comfortable once we fixed up benches and tables to eat on. The Mess Section constantly worked to improve their area and even talked me into creating a sign for them that dubbed the place "The Desert Oasis."

We were lucky to have a bunch of good cooks. They made the best out of what we were issued in the way of food, which consisted largely of t-rats. These were large aluminum trays of food designed to be steam-heated and meant to feed ten soldiers. T-rat entrees might consist of chili macaroni, chicken cacciatore, lasagna, roast beef, ham and eggs, or any one of a number of gourmet adventures. These were not very popular with the troops, who often complained of their "blandness." Even something like t-rat hamburgers failed to make the grade… this entree consisted of pre-cooked patties, buns, MRE cheese that you squeezed out of foil packets and condiments. McDonalds had nothing to worry about.

Our food was occasionally augmented by entrees in microwavable containers. Unfortunately, we had no way to microwave them... unless we used the HIPIR.[20] Fortunately they could be heated by immersing in hot water. Fortunately for us, the cooks were also provided with canned vegetables and fruit and the ingredients necessary to make some food from scratch: bread, brownies, cake, etc. Sergeant First Class Yelle, our Mess Sergeant, created a shrimp sauce concoction which was awesome over rice.

We'd get local packaged foods too, like soda and cookies. Coke and Pepsi tasted just the same as back home, just with all that squiggly writing on it. German-made Zit Cola was OK, although the name was a bit of a put-off for Americans. However, the only cookies we ever got were banana cookies.

Banana cookies are definitely an acquired taste.

We discovered later on that there was actually a large assortment of cookies available "on the economy:" orange, custard, etc., but our battalion supply had a bad habit of sorting through what was sent to them, keeping what they liked and shipping the rest to the batteries.

This problem with our battalion supply was aptly illustrated by an incident which took place before Thanksgiving. The Big Top was used to house weight sets for soldiers who wanted to exercise with them and as a good place for them to "hang out" when not on duty. The weight set was one of thousands donated by an American company for use by troops in the field and distributed by the regular supply channels. They were highly appreciated by soldiers.

One day we received word that the battalion had been provided with seven television/VCR sets, also donated by an American company. This was greeted with much enthusiasm as some soldiers had video tapes that they brought with them others knew they could ask for others to be sent in packages from home.

Seven sets made absolute sense: each of the three Hawk battery had two self-contained sites and the battalion site made seven. But when a vehicle was sent to pick up our sets only one was available.

Lt. Pace picked up the phone and did some checking. He found that the other Hawk batteries each got two... we were the only battery to get just one set. But when Pace called battalion supply they tried to explain to him that 2+2+2+1 equals six, not seven.

---

[20] The HIPIR actually was capable of microwaving objects at close range, which is why we had a lot of safety protocols regarding its use. No one wants to get a tan from the inside out.

Pace wasn't one to be put off. He went to battalion in person and discovered that two sets had been kept at battalion. One was set up in the supply tent for their own private use.

Our XO went ballistic. Battalion supply tried to justify keeping the set while denying one to our other isolated site. After rocking the boat we got both the sets we had been promised.

Selfish incidents like this did little to endear our soldiers at the missile sites to the support personnel at the battalion. They often got the impression that the headquarters didn't give a damn.

Telephones gave us a lifeline back home via "morale calls," but a very thin one. You had to be close to phone center, and not everyone was. You also had to stand in line for maybe a couple of hours to make a short 15-minute call. The time difference didn't help either.

Mail was undoubtedly the most important factor in our morale. Someone who has never lived thousands of miles from home in a primitive and isolated environment cannot imagine how important mail was to us. In the days before email and blogs and cell phones it was letters that gave us our link to the outside world, it was these envelopes from home which helped us get through the day. Letters reminded us that there was a world outside Saudi Arabia and provided daily proof that our loved ones were still thinking of us.

Mail was picked up on a daily basis from battalion and was distributed by section to individuals. I looked forward to letters from my parents and from friends. "Goody boxes" were a great morale booster: books, candy, canned food, socks, film, shoelaces, writing paper, magazines, newspapers, powdered drink mixes, peanuts, batteries, hacky sacks, holiday cards, envelopes, toothpaste, Bibles, pens, shampoo, notebooks, etc. were all sent in boxes. There were some things which were forbidden by General Order #1, however: pornography (such as Playboy or that rather explicit article in Cosmopolitan), alcohol (do not put Jim Beam[21] in a Listerine bottle… you're not fooling anybody) and guns (we have plenty, thank you). The greatest value of boxes was it gave you something to share with others.

There was mail from a quarter we never even considered, and that was from the American People as a whole. Americans showed their support for us by sending letters addressed to "Any Soldier" and "To A Deserving Soldier," as did packages addressed the same way. Whenever I had any doubts about being in Arabia, about the job I was doing or about being so far away from home, I would read one of those letters and be encouraged by the confidence expressed in it

---

[21] The penalty for possessing Jim Beam in the Kingdom of Saudi Arabia is death.

DAYDREAMS ALL WRAPPED UP IN ONE.

and touched by some stranger I would never meet taking the time to write and send it.

These were all the positive aspects of mail. Of course, not every bit of news was good and mail could be a *negative* morale factor. Some soldiers got letters about problems at home which they could do nothing about except worry. Others got "Dear John" letters from girlfriends or wives, and in at least one case we had a female soldier get a "Dear Jane" letter. But even with the occasional bad news the mail was vital.

Books came in the mail too. I read books about Iraq, Sherlock Holmes stories, science fiction, all kinds of stuff. It was a rare day when you didn't see someone off-duty reading. It was the only escape most of us had from the desert.

Newspapers were distributed with the mail: Stars and Stripes, unit papers and Saudi English-language publications. Newspapers from the States would also arrive in "care boxes." This gave us a better idea of what was going on in the world than just the info channels and radio were providing.

We began to get paid and I got the job of Battery Pay Officer. At first we were paid authorized only $50 in U.S. currency per soldier per month, which would be deducted from the soldiers regular pay. A lot of soldiers felt this wasn't much, but then again there wasn't much to spend the money on. Sure, there were field PXs, but none of them were convenient for us to get to. The Saudis accepted dollars but village shops were even rarer than the PX, and they rarely stocked items wanted or needed by GIs. Still, having money on you had a way of making you feel more secure somehow.

The job of Pay officer came close to driving me crazy. Aside from the paperwork involved and the time it took the job had the additional downside of making me come up short $20 every time I did it. And if the paperwork for just drawing the money and turning in the difference was a headache, I didn't want to think about what was involved in reporting a shortage. I decided to make up the $20 out of my own pay. I never did figure out where that money went.

One soldier was in difficult circumstances due to an Army Catch-22. Even though he had worked alongside the rest of us to deploy, did everything he was supposed to do and was sweating alongside the rest of us, he was officially a deserter. Why? Because the unit was placed on "stop-loss," cancelling all reassignments, schools, leaves, etc. before we left. This soldier had orders for Germany but he went to Saudi Arabia instead. So, when he failed to show up at the unit waiting for him in Germany they filled out a DD553, Deserter/Absentee Wanted By The Armed Forces. Shortly after that he stopped getting paid.

I drove him on a run to the Ice Palace, where 11th ADA Brigade had its Forward Headquarters. The building actually was an ice-making facility and while it must have still been over 100 degrees outside it was maybe 68 inside. Soldiers were wearing shorts and t-shirts. I think we disturbed the harmony of the place, showing up fully armed and wearing our battle-rattle.

The staff didn't seem very helpful to us. Of course, it may have just been that the drive in 100 degree heat while wearing DCUs might have affected our attitude when we entered the personnel office. They claimed the problem could not be fixed in Saudi Arabia. I later thought to myself that, as a "deserter," the soldier could have turned himself in at the embassy in Riyadh, got a U.S. marshal to escort him back to Fort Bliss. THEN he could get it all sorted out. To his credit, he stuck with us even though it was causing hardship to his family.

After a hard day in the desert nothing beat a shower. We were allocated three-stall wooden units which must have been slapped together by the Army Engineers, with walls that came up maybe five feet high. Each shower unit had a small tank mounted on the roof and we rigged up an immersion heater from the Mess Section to heat up water in an unused trash can and then pump it into the tank. It worked reasonably well.

Once the hot water situation was dealt with the next problem to be addressed was how to schedule showers so that the females could have privacy and vice-versa. A schedule was created but it only provided a 30-minute "window" for the females to take a shower every night but some of them complained that this was not sufficient. However, with only four of the 60 soldiers at Radar Hill being women the BC felt that this was sufficient.

One evening I walked out to the showers, put my towel and my kit in one of the stalls and got undressed. Someone else was in the center stall but I paid no attention as I began to wash the sweat off of me.

Then I happened to look over at the other stall and noticed for the first time that the other soldier had shoulder-length hair.

"Sanchez?" I asked. Aghast, I quickly reached for my watch to check the time; I was in a near panic at the thought of having made a mistake and using the showers during the females' allotted block of time. But the watch showed that I was in the right.

I tried to sound indignant. "Sanchez, what are you doing here?"

"Sir, as long as I don't see anything of yours and you don't see anything of mine, it's OK." And she went back to taking her shower.

SHOWERS WERE A VERY BIG DEAL
IN THE DESERT. WHILE ADA UNITS
WERE OPEN TO FEMALES MANY OF
THE RULES DEFINITELY DID NOT
FAVOR THEM.

She was right: the height of the wooden partitions gave us privacy, so long as neither of us took the trouble to get closer. And in the dark it would have been hard to see anything anyway.

As far as I know, that was the only instance of males and females taking showers at the same time at Radar Hill.

Laundry was one of our biggest problems. There was no convenient way to do it in the desert, although after a couple of months the Army did thoughtfully send us a couple of washbasins to do it by hand. Detergent was provided in "convenience packs:" big boxes of sundry items like shampoo, soap and toothpaste. We rigged up racks to dry clothes in the sun but it only took a short gust of wind to get sand on everything… then you'd have to wash the clothes all over again.

Eventually we had a laundry service provided by the Quartermasters. It did a good job but they took several days to get clothes back to you… and every once in a while they would lose a uniform. In Saudi Arabia that was bad news as there was almost no way to get a replacement.

Physical Training was still done, even though it was difficult to free soldiers from their other duties to perform it. Captain Fletcher wanted us ready for whatever was to come.

At first, PT was done in the morning but that was no good because the showers weren't available. Instead, we started exercising in the afternoon prior to dinner. Most of the regimen wasn't bad, but the BC took charge of the run personally and Fletcher would run at a moderate pace but could keep it up seemingly forever. We would run towards the nearby highway but no matter how long you ran it never seemed to get closer. Passing the occasional dead camel along the route did nothing to bolster our enthusiasm.

Except for the holidays and the infrequent Iraqi "surprises" this was pretty much life for those of us in Bravo Battery.

4. BAGHDAD BETTY

Thanksgiving started out with a routine check on the missile system. We did some target transfers with Patriot but had issues with the IFF. Lt. Col. Thomson, the Deputy Brigade Command of 11th ADA and the officer slated to take command of our battalion at some unspecified point in the future, stopped by and stuck his head in the control van. He looked around and left without really saying anything.

Sergeant Young turned back from the door. "I wonder what HE wanted."

I shrugged and checked the IFF again.

Maybe it was just because we were so far from home or maybe it was because we were doing without the kind of food we took for granted in the States, but Thanksgiving 1990 was one of the best I remember.

Our cooks went to extra lengths to provide a truly outstanding meal. The Army might have provided all the ingredients (turkey, roast beef, corn on the cob, mashed potatoes, stuffing, gravy, fresh salad and illicit ham) but it was the cooks who put it all together for us like home-made.

There was plenty of soda and milk to go along with the meal, as well as tangerines, grapes, apples, and oranges. It was more food than we could really eat in one sitting.

Not all of our soldiers were with us, however. Our battery sent a couple of our soldiers to eat Thanksgiving dinner with President George H.W. Bush, who made a special trip to be with us on this holiday. Of course, by the time you when you have so many units in one place a soldier here and a soldier there turns into hundreds when you get them together to eat turkey with the President, but it really meant a lot to us that he took time from his working schedule and his own family to be with us.

Most of soldiers from the second platoon were allowed to come over to Radar Hill so they could enjoy the full spread rather than have the meal delivered to them in sealed canisters. After dinner we had a football game in true American fashion: split up the group (battery) into two camps in a mild fight to the death. In this case it was First Platoon against Second Platoon. A playing field was laid out in the sand next to our mess trailer. We used diesel fuel make the lines.

51

Thanksgiving at the Scud Bowl game. It was 1st Platoon versus 2nd Platoon at Radar Hill. At upper left you can see the Big Top.

Christmas Day, 1990. Inside the Big Top we celebrated with a good dinner and good company.

Both teams played well and it was a spirited game. Someone brought out a radio and started playing rock and roll music while we cheered for our respective platoons. Some soldiers even managed to find chairs to relax in the whole scene had a surreal quality to it, like something from an episode of MASH[22]. I half-expected Hawkeye or Col. Potter to turn up.

AFN was a welcome source of news and music but for sheer comedy nothing beat Radio Baghdad, Saddam's official propaganda station and the self-appointed "Voice of Peace."

Radio Baghdad played some good music on occasion but clearly whoever was in charge over there had no idea how Americans think. This rendered their propaganda ineffective (at least to us, their primary audience) but provided all sorts of unintended entertainment. The music included selections from Cher, Queen, Sting, and other musical talent popular at the time but mostly pop music ("What does Saddam have against Country and Western?" Chief Dungy would ask). They even played Stairway to Heaven once... the Led Zeppelin version, not the 1960 Neil Sedaka hit.

The English broadcasts we could pick up on shortwave weren't even particularly enthusiastic. The male announcer on Radio Baghdad delivered his scripted news reports in a monotone. These scripts never attempted to create division among the various members of the Coalition, which would have been a logical goal and perhaps even an attainable one. Instead, the news broadcasts merely parroted the Ba'athist regime's position: Kuwait was a part of Iraq now, that it ALWAYS should have been a part of Iraq, and it would continue to be part of Iraq no matter what the Americans do. They did not address what role the KUWAITIS might have in determining what would happen to Kuwait and they certainly didn't say anything about Iraq's cowardly hostage taking.

"Iraq dismissed Western media reports that it would make a surprise move before January 15th and withdraw from the Province of Kuwait," went one "News and Reviews" broadcast, "a statement issued following a joint meeting of the Iraqi Revolutionary Command Council and the Arab Ba'ath Socialist Party Regional Command have branded such reports as 'sick thinking that exists only in the minds of the planners of Evil and their dubious circle.'"

That's telling them.

The Iraqis also made sure to talk about stateside peace demonstrations in their broadcasts. It was remarkable to me how a country that had just used naked military force to overrun and brutally occupy one neighbor and threaten another could be so happy about peace protestors. They mentioned, in steady

---

[22] Only without Major Burns, thank goodness.

THE DAILY DOSE
OF PROPAGANDA...
DEFINITELY NOT
HABIT-FORMING

tone of voice, how peace protestors climbed over the White House fence and dumped red paint in the fountain. But if they thought that was going to bother us, they were mistaken. We knew from our letters and from newspapers that most of the American people were on OUR side.

The only enthusiasm the male Iraqi broadcaster would display was when making the initial or the final announcement. In a sinister voice he would say "Our transmission continues for seven hours daily, from 11860 kilohertz on the shortwave band, 1135 kilohertz on the medium wave band, and 540 kilohertz on the medium wave band." There would be a short musical interlude of Arab music, then in a menacing tone he would say "The Voice of Peace comes to you daily, between 2 and 5 PM…. OUR local time, YOUR local time."

"What are they trying to do?" Staff Sergeant Lacher asked once. "Scare us because we're in the same time zone?"

And in the ultimate bit of hypocrisy, he would end with "For all you peace lovers everywhere, this is the Voice of Peace." Staff Sergeant Lacher called the music that followed THAT gem the Goat Song, and even came up with lyrics for the Arabic music: "Oh yes, this is a very nice goat, oh yes, this is my very favorite goat…"

Baghdad Betty was the one who tried to discourage us with little propaganda one-liners such as: "Is it another day of festivities for you (meaning Thanksgiving) or just another sad day?," "My friends, you had better prepare to die.," "It won't be easy for the American States to win a war… without shedding blood.," and "American soldiers fight other people's wars." Each zinger was followed up with bizarrely upbeat Muzak.

"Dear American soldier," I remember hearing once, "are you still waiting to die for a cheap barrel of oil?" A soldier sitting in the CP snorted "Right now I'd kill for a beer!"

The day after Thanksgiving our platoon went on full alert, the first of many times we would do so.

At noon I was running firing functions on the Hawk system and was about to simulate a launch when the Air Defense Warning Light went from "White" (no attack is underway) to "Yellow" (attack is possible) with no advance notice.

"Hold one." I told the crew over the headset. I switched to "hot" so I could speak to the Tactical Director. "This is Bravo-One, Zero-Six. What's going on?"

There was no response. I tried again. "Zero-Six, this is Bravo One. Why have we gone to Yellow?" Still no response. "Can any station hear me?" Silence.

It was clear that the secure voicelink was out, and at the worst possible time. The datalink was still working, which was how we got the message that the ADW status had changed, but without voice commands we wouldn't have the precision that we normally relied on.

I took the initiative and acted on the assumption that an attack might soon be underway and we were already being subjected to jamming or communications sabotage. I hit the PCP's siren twice and turned to Sergeant Stake, the commo guy. "Try to raise the BTOC, find out what's going on."

While he fiddled with the radio stack and his own headset I began to run through all the readiness checks in the van. "This is the Crew Chief," I heard over the headset, "what's our status?"

"Right now go through it like it's Blazing Skies. I'm trying to get hold of Higher now."

PFC Meister came on line. "This is the CWAR. What's our status?"

"Blazing Skies."

"Permission to go to local?"

"Go."

I watched the status board above the main console. CWAR dropped. No commo with HIPIR, but we fixed that quickly enough. Sergeant Stake came over from the stack. "Sir, BTOC says that one of the fire units has hostile tracks."

"Level Two Check complete." I noted. "CWAR report to the van. HIPIR report to the van."

It took no time at all for the crew to come in, complete their respective checks and take their places within the van. None of us said anything. We all knew that this could be it.

Whitmire and Pace arrived and wanted to know what was going on. I gave them a quick rundown of the situation, but there were still no targets on the radar screen.

Sergeant stake was still listening in on the back channel to headquarters. He lowered the headset, which he was holding to one ear. "BTOC says permission is granted to hook up the missiles."

By now I figured it would go this far. "Crew Chief," I called over the headset, "arm all missiles, remove all safeties, and connect the umbilicals."

There was no response. "Did you get that, Crew Chief?"

"Roger," the J-Box Operator responded. "They're on their way to the launchers."

Sergeant Stokely was my radar operator for that shift. His efforts on his headset finally got him through to the TD. We exchanged headsets.

Before I could even speak to the TD the Crew Chief came back on. "Everything is armed."

"Remote in the launchers," I told him. "And let me know when everyone is uprange."

A minute later he came on again: "Launchers One, Two, and Three remoted in. Safety keys in hand. The downrange area is clear."

Joe Pace nudged me. "Better make sure you have a reload crew available."

I nodded but mentally kicked myself for not already doing that. "Crew Chief, do we have a reload ready?"

"Roger, crew is prepping now."

"Don't get excited," Joe said. "Just take orders from the ICC."

Again I nodded.

The "Missile Ready" lights came up on the TDECC. I reached for the "Arm-Safe-Test" switch. "Taking the system to 'Arm.'" I announced, as per training. I then turned the switch. At this point the system was fully operational and prepared to engage and destroy any target selected.

Except that there were no targets. I could not see the hostiles picked up by others on my scope. The Alpha was on, but either was not indicating or was showing "Unknown Aircraft." This could be because the Iraqis had modified the avionics.

The aircraft in question were MiG-25 Foxbats.[23]

How did we know this? Our intelligence folks did an assessment based on how the aircraft were flying and the point-of-origin. Since the aircraft had been tracked after lifting off from an Iraqi airfield an assumption was made that it had to be one of three aircraft known to be operating out of that airfield. The altitude and speed narrowed it down as well but the fact that the aircraft were willing to fly into the teeth of our missile defenses pretty much clinched it. Only the Foxbat could fly into the net at altitude and survive, thanks to its top speed of Mach 3. And even then it had to be very, very careful.

The MiGs were either trying to fly a recon mission or attempting to trick us into turning on everything in the air defense net and maybe even firing missiles at them. There was a rumor that this had already happened earlier, when the Saudis were tricked into firing at Iraqi Foxbats flying along the border. MiG-25s can't exactly outrun Hawk missiles but if they have a long enough lead the missile engine will run out of fuel before it can reach them.

We stood by, waiting for our orders. From what we could find out through our link with BTOC a group of aircraft had been detected by Alpha Battery, 3rd Battalion 43rd ADA, one of the Patriot fire units in Task Force

---

[23] Saddam later buried some of these planes in the desert for safekeeping; makes perfect sense to me.

IRAQI
FOXBAT

Scorpion. The planes were in Iraqi airspace, headed over Kuwait and approaching Saudi airspace.

Finally, the word came over commo channels: "The bogies have turned back."

I wasted no time standing down. "Taking the system back to 'Safe,'" then over the headset: "J-box, take Launchers One, Two and Three to 'Safe.'"

"One, Two and Three in 'Safe.'" Came the correct response.

"Crew Chief, proceed to take all launchers to 'Local,' disconnect the umbilicals, place the missiles in 'Safe' and replace the safety keys."

"Roger."

I removed the headset once the situation was in hand. Joe and Staff Sergeant Mitchell were both in a good mood because our fire platoon had risen to the occasion so quickly and purposefully. They left the van smiling.

Sergeant Stokely watched them leave. Now that the burden of locking on to and destroying an actual target was lifted off his shoulders he muttered "Well, at least SOMEONE's happy."

If Saddam was trying to spoof us then he failed on that account. We weren't falling for the old waste-hawk-missiles-on-a-supersonic-Foxbat trick.

On a different day I walked in on some of the soldiers as they were gathered around the TVM display in the PCP. Everyone suddenly dispersed when they saw me.

I looked at the screen and saw that the TVM was aimed at the field hospital. A closer look and I could see that the picture was focused on the outdoor showers.

I looked at the crew. "Watching the nurses?"

The radar operator reset the camera and shut it off. "Yes, Sir."

I believe I said something about using the HIPIR as a high-tech (or at least medium-tech) peeping tom device. I also added that someone was bound to get suspicious when they saw the antenna frequently aimed in the direction of the showers. Then I asked "Did you see anything?"

"No, Sir." He replied. "Damn sides are too high."

Captain Fletcher took us on a road trip. Actually, he took the RSOP teams on a route reconnaissance in support of the Big Move everyone knew was coming. By now the Coalition was secure in its defense of Saudi Arabia but it was also clear that Saddam intended to try to "wait out" the UN sanctions, no doubt thinking that the Coalition would eventually fall apart from inaction.

The word was passed down to us that VII Corps was on its way from Germany to join the Coalition. VII Corps' 1st Armored Division, 3rd Armored

Division and 2nd Armored Cavalry Regiment represented an enormous amount of fighting power. Augmented by the 1st Cavalry Division and the 1st Infantry Division already in theater and it was hard to imagine anything that could stop them. Clearly we were NOT going to fight a war of attrition. The fact that we were doing route recon to the Kuwaiti border backed up that perception.

Cpt. Fletcher led the way in B6, his HMMWV, while I followed in B103 with Sergeant Young driving. Lieutenants Williams and Riley and their driver pulled in between my vehicle and the BC when we rendezvoused at the highway, then all three vehicles headed north.

I followed the route on my tourist map and counted myself damn lucky to even have that. Maps of any kind were in short supply and this one at least told me the names of the towns and where the roads went. I joked on the way up with Young, who was good company. We passed what I later found out was an ancient Portuguese fort. It was in ruins and fenced off by the Saudis, another reminded of how far back history goes in this part of the world.

We also passed Charlie Battery's forward position ("Pet Sematary Site") which was positioned near a supply dump. Our little convoy reached the village of as -Nariyah and turned west. After driving in that direction for a while, Fletcher had us turn around and we headed east, passing through the village again.

The route we now passed through was even more desolate than the area to the South, if that was possible. There were no signs of any other American units. Arab drivers zipped around us, oblivious to posted speed limits or posted traffic warnings.

Off in the distance to the East the desert seemed to change. "Isn't that the Gulf?" I asked.

Sergeant Young looked but shrugged. "We aren't supposed to be going near the Gulf."

But sure enough, we were soon within a mile of the beach. We were also passing signs: "Kuwait, 212Km." I figured there was some sort of a change in plans.

We passed a Crotale surface-to-air missile battery at an airfield. Nearby aircraft, including a C-130, had United Arab Emirates markings. "Kuwait City, 190Km."

At first we passed a few Arab civilians and kids giving us the "V for Victory" sign. After a while there was no one on the road but us. "Kuwait City, 160Km."

I shook my head. "When it gets down to double digits I'm calling the BC to find out what's going on, radio silence or no radio silence."

Cpt. Fletcher fine-tuning the layout of the Radar Hill Site as he stands near the CWAR antenna. Note the rocks around the hill; this made some site improvements difficult.

I shot this with the SLR during a recon run. After we were in Saudi Arabia for a while routine duties meant hats instead of helmets and a weapon and promask instead of all-out battle-rattle.

150 kilometers from Kuwait City and just a few miles South of Khafji we pulled over. Captain Fletcher got out of his vehicle wearing his flak vest and pistol rig. "The map is useless. Let's eat lunch and then we'll start back." He looked around. "Judging from the terrain, it won't really make a difference where we set up."[24]

The place was flat, and as I almost found out the hard way, inhabited by scorpions. Even though I brought my camera there wasn't anything worth getting pictures of.

We turned our vehicles around and headed back. At as-Nariyah we stopped and shopped around a bit. It was the first chance I had to see an Arab village.

The people were friendly and gladly took U.S. dollars. I bought a case of RC Cola (I was amazed to see some there). Aside from the Arabic writing, the cans were taller and thinner than the ones we were used to.

We also ran into kids. We tried to give them some MREs but they weren't interested in them (word must have gotten around fast) but they did like chemlites. I guess they were fascinated by the glowing sticks but we simply had none to spare. "Sorry, kids" I told them. "No chemlites."

Our party got back together at the vehicles and prepared to finish the trip. I passed out some of my RCs and Captain Fletcher handed out some "near-beer."

We stood at the road intersection talking amongst ourselves when a white car pulled up and an Arab in traditional dress got out and started having words with a nearby police officer and pointing at his machine. The car was in real bad shape and must have just been in an accident: part of the front end was badly mangled.

After a minute or two of animated conversation between the police officer and the civilian the owner of the car got back in and proceeded to drive south... one front wheel wobbling erratically.

"Do you think he'll make it?" I wondered out loud.

Captain Fletcher grinned. "I wouldn't be surprised if he passes somebody in that thing."

As November turned into December we continued to make improvements around the Radar Hill site to make it a little more livable. Some of the improvements simply involved getting civilian blankets, pillows, camp furniture, etc.

---

[24] This whole thing might have been part of a deception plan. Many operations took place prior to the Ground War in order to convince the Iraqis that the Coalition effort would go right through Kuwait.

We also did more of the hand-made signs for various tents. "The Abyss," "Hawk Manor," "Doc's Place," and "Scudd Inn" were some of the signs in our area, while battalion had "Dew Drop Inn," Warhawk Infirmary," Camel Lot," "Ba'ath House" and "Maintenance Has the Tool." Many of these had their own artwork and it was a way of using up untapped creative energy. For my creative energy I kept working on cartoons.

We also built improved bunkers with overhead cover. We weren't very concerned about any aircraft coming in and bombing us, but we did worry about Saddam's own "secret weapon:" scuds. Scud bunkers became a regular feature for just about any military site. And for good reason.

"SCUD ALERT! SCUD ALERT! THIS IS NOT A DRILL!"

I grabbed my gear and ran towards the far side of the hill. Lt. Whitmire was on duty in the van so I wasn't needed there. Lt. Pace's voice continued to call out his warning in between the noise that was our "scud alarm."

I threw myself into the main scud bunker, which was a sandbagged rock overhang that our soldiers had dug out with the scooploader and by hand. We hoped it was capable of taking a direct hit by a scud missile. Hell, I think I would have been happy if it could take a near-miss without collapsing.

The scuds posed a threat for two reasons: because of their range and, ironically, their inaccuracy. The Soviets who sold them to Saddam weren't too worried about the accuracy part because they were intended to send chemical and nuclear weapons raining down on the "NATO warmongers."

Saddam knew a good thing when he saw one and using rockets to hit a big target like a city with a conventional warhead was a good thing in his book. Unfortunately for him, during the Iran-Iraq War it turned out that the most lucrative targets were all out of range of the standard scud. The Iraqis needed more range.

Designing a better missile from scratch was either uneconomical or beyond Iraq's technological abilities or both. In any case, a simpler and cheaper solution was to take existing scud missiles, cut the fuselage and lengthen it. Internally, the fuel and oxidizer tanks were lengthened as well, allowing the engine to burn longer and the warhead was reduced, making it a bit lighter once the fuel burned off. Not a terribly sophisticated approach but it worked: the al-Hussein model could reach 650 kilometers and the al-Abbas up to 800 kilometers.[25] Regardless of model, all Iraqi missiles were called "scuds."

---

[25] The renegade Canadian scientist Gerald Bull is credited with providing Saddam the technical know-how to redesign his scuds. Bull was the mastermind behind the Supergun as well, a project he said he was going to use to shoot satellites into space but which was "aimed" at Israel.

IRAQ ATTACKS!
BUT ACCURACY IS A PROBLEM.

The price paid in this process was accuracy: with a conventional warhead the bastardized scuds could only be used against a city or large military facility, where an impact almost ANYWHERE would destroy SOMETHING and maybe kill some people. The scuds were terrorist, not military, weapons. And as such, they might be aimed at a division headquarters... and land on a Hawk missile site instead.

It was now December 2nd. The United Nations had set a deadline for Iraq to withdraw from Kuwait and it was obvious to everyone that failure to do so would result in some very heavy military action. It occurred to me that Saddam might be responding to the deadline by launching a preemptive attack while he still had the means. A desperate strategy, but Iraq was in a desperate situation.

We were sitting in the bunker in varying degrees of chemical protection: pants, jackets, boots and gloves, but EVERYONE at the very least had their mask on. Many did not have their flak vests and some didn't have a MOPP suit with them at all. We proceeded to suit up and the NCOs sent soldiers in small groups to get their gear if they neglected to bring it with them.

Over a hand-held radio the CP ordered us to unmask and standby for target verification. Space Command satellites, originally placed in orbit to detect the launch of Soviet or Chinese ICBMs, "saw" the heat of scud rocket motors rising from southern Iraq. An alert was sent to Space Command Headquarters in Colorado, which then relayed it via satellite to our air defense net in Saudi Arabia, which was then disseminated down to our level. Now in our little corner of the world there were 30 of us waiting to find out if a missile was going to renter the atmosphere somewhere over our heads.

Staff Sergeant Hurt floated the idea of getting a missile reload ready "just in case." I thought about it and it did seem like the prudent thing to do. What if the scud was a diversion and the REAL attack would be via airstrike? In fact, MiG-23s and MiG-27s could even now be on their way in an attempt to take out our missile sites and unravel the air defense net.

Besides, I knew that whatever happened I didn't want to be in a hole when the enemy flew over. "I'm getting my vest!" I told Hurt.

"You'd better RUN, lieutenant!" he replied as I headed over to my tent. I grabbed my despised flak vest (it was too heavy to wear comfortably but too light to protect you) and ran for the missile pallets. Williams was operating the transloader and Staff Sergeant Tijerina stood by to assist.

The transloader was having problems hooking up with the three missiles we were trying to pick up. We settled on getting two of three and I was just putting my glasses back on when there was a huge "BOOM!" overhead.

THE DEFINITION OF
"TIGHT CONTROL"

"What the Hell?!" I yelled out loud. I looked up and even though I only saw it for a fraction of a second my brain identified the aircraft as two Panavia Tornadoes, RAF markings. My mind took stock of the bombs and missiles loaded on the one directly overhead. It was one of the strangest things I've ever experienced: even though the aircraft was above us for only a fraction of a second it was as if I had a photo of the plane's underbelly in my head. In a moment both planes were gone, heading north.

Looking around the floor of the desert from Radar Hill I noticed for the first time the number of aircraft heading SOUTH. I was sure that the war had just begun.

We moved the transloader to a position where it was shielded from the launch effects if we had to fire but close enough to bring them over real quick when the time came.

It all turned out to be saber-rattling. Saddam fired three missiles from Iraq that day, at 30 –minute intervals, but all of them impacted in Iraqi territory. Either he was trying to gauge our reaction or else he was playing some sort of mind game.

The scuds did not worry us as much as what might be on them. Saddam might put chemical or biological agents in the warheads. So far, that seemed to be beyond Saddam's technical expertise but the more people got to know this tin-plated Third-World dictator the less you could doubt he WOULD if he could. So we kept our chemical protection gear close and took our anthrax shots and waited. The only thing I could see being accomplished by the Missiles of December is that it made everyone take the threat that much more seriously.

5. CAMEL COMMANDO

Saddam had either come to the conclusion that he no longer needed the "human shields" being held hostage in Iraq or else realized the damage to his image was far worse than the marginal advantage they gave him. But while he let Europeans and Americans go he kept another 2,000,000 Kuwaitis hostage. The Coalition was making plans to spring them as well.

Staff Sergeants Mitchell, Tijerina, Hurt and Reyes were all promoted to Sergeant First Class. Lt. Col. Kilgore came down to our site to pin their new rank on. They were pinned by the battalion commander as the orders were read in front of the troops.

Afterwards they did pushups as soldiers poured jerry cans of water over them. This Army tradition was symbolic of the "washing away" of the NCO's or officer's previous mistakes and giving him a chance to start over at his new rank. Of course, it was also fun for privates to get away with dumping freezing cold water on their leaders.

We celebrated with "near beer." Non-alcoholic beer[26] was available in Saudi Arabia and I drove to a nearby village to try to find some in a general store. An old Saudi man handed me a pamphlet in English, something about "How To Become a Muslim In One Easy Step," which I took graciously. I didn't bother to share with the guy my affinity for pulled pork sandwiches.

Inside the place I wasn't having any luck as the shop owner didn't speak any English. Nor did he *sprecht deutsch* or *parlez vous francais*.

Then a Saudi entered the store, wearing traditional dress. "Can I help you?" He asked, in perfect English.

"Yes, we're trying to find non-alcoholic beer." I told him.

"Ah," he replied. "I will show you where to find it."

The beer was hidden in a steel freezer in the back. I thanked the man for his help and told him "You know, your English is very good."

He smiled back at me. "I went to school in the United States. In Ohio!"

"Oh really? I went to school in Ohio."

He stood up proudly and said "I went to The Ohio State University."

I nodded. "Yeah, well, I went to Wright State University..."

All of a sudden his throat gurgled and he spat on the floor" "Ptooey!"

There was an awkward silence. "I get that a lot." I finally said.

---

[26] The penalty for selling alcoholic beer in the Kingdom of Saudi Arabia is death.

Our soldiers rarely saw any of the local animals, if for no other reason than there were very few to see in the desert. But one exception was the cobra which suddenly appeared in the middle of the site.

It made its presence known to the mechanics driving the wrecker one day by gathering itself up and then striking the front bumper. When the machine did not drop dead (!) or retreat the cobra arched back and struck again. And again.

While it was fixated on killing the truck a mechanic warily got out of the cab and grabbed a shovel. He worked his way behind it and began whacking it in the back of the head. The cobra, for its part, would not let the shovel blows distract it from the idea of killing the truck.

In the end the cobra lost this battle of wills. And its life.

As things got into a routine we had a problem with our senior generator mechanic.

The disguised Alpha sensor was sitting out near the lieutenant's tent. It looked just like an ordinary Army generator, except for the fact that we never ran it, we had surrounded it with concertina wire and it was exceedingly clean.

Officially, we told everyone it was an emergency generator but that it was not to be run as part of the normal system configuration. This story didn't hold water when one of the REAL generators would drop sometimes and we would refuse to power up the "emergency generator" and reroute the power.

So one day I'm talking to someone and there goes this generator mechanic, heading straight for the sensor with a clipboard in his hand. I suddenly realized where he was going. "Sergeant! What are you doing?"

"I'm going to go check out the generator, Sir."

"That generator is off-limits, Sergeant!" I yelled. All the man would have to do would be open up the front of the machine and he would KNOW it wasn't a real generator.

So we came up with a better story. If it became necessary, we would swear the mechanic to secrecy and inform him that the generator was actually a prototype miniature nuclear reactor. It could power the entire system by itself. Unfortunately, the shielding wasn't that good and THAT's why we kept it powered down most of the time and why only a few people were allowed to go near it at all. I don't recall if we ever had to USE this cover story but I do remember that the sergeant stopped insisting on seeing daily maintenance checks from us or from checking it out himself.[27]

---

[27] While I kept a journal from the Gulf War I have to rely on my memory for Alpha, as we were not allowed to mention the system in notes. Even in the school all notes and drawings were secured following the course.

THE ALPHA SENSOR WAS
INGENIOUSLY DISGUISED AS
PART OF THE ELECTRICAL
SUPPLY.

Tijerina and I stopped on a pay run once, going over to a camel herder we saw eating his lunch near the sand "road." I gestured with my camera to see if he was all right with me taking his picture and he didn't seem to mind. In fact, he enthusiastically grabbed me and smiled and muttered something in Arabic. I told Tijerina "Take the picture, already!"

I took pictures of Tijerina with the guy as well. Then I remembered we had some excess oranges in the vehicle. Both of our sites had plenty enough for anyone who wanted them. They were just going to go bad if we didn't give them to someone. "Hey, let's see if he doesn't want to take some of these oranges off our hands."

Oh, the guy LOVED the oranges. So we gave him some water as well. We had more than enough bottled water to spare and he was happy as a clam when we finally left him.

When we arrived back at the site we came in just ahead of the Battery Commander. He had info for us from a briefing at battalion headquarters and the senior leaders met at the CP. A lot of the information was purely administrative, some of it was situational, and finally he added some timely intel: "If you see any camel herders in this area stay away from them. G-2 has reason to believe that they are really Iraqi infiltrators who have crossed the border disguised as local Bedouins. These commandos are actually roaming around to get information on our units in order to report back to their forces via radio."

"Sir….?" Tijerina began speaking quietly next to me.

"Shut up." I hissed

"Commandos did this same kind of thing just before they invaded Kuwait. They had radios hidden in their camel saddles."

"Sir…?" I heard Tijerina again.

"Shut up!" I whispered.

"G-2 doesn't think they'll hang around here very long, anyways. They have no access to supplies this far from their lines."

Tijerina and I just looked at each other.

"G-2 is leaving them alone so they can continue to report what we want them to report."

All I could think of was the phrase "Aiding the enemy" and how it would sound at the court-martial.[28]

---

[28] Article 104 of the Uniform Code of Military Justice (Aiding the Enemy): Any person who aids, or attempts to aid, the enemy with arms, ammunition, supplies, money, or other things; or without proper authority, knowingly harbors or protects or gives intelligence to or communicates or corresponds with or holds any intercourse with the

On December 15th we were put on Scud Alert again. Or more accurately, a scud warning. No scud was actually launched but one of our sources detected a Russian weather radar associated with the missile. This radar would track balloons specially launched into the upper atmosphere to provide weather data. This was entered into a computer and correction would be made to increase the missile's accuracy. In theory, anyway.

It was after 1900 and already dark. I waited with Captain Fletcher, Lt. Pace and Staff Sergeant Lacher in the CP. I got bored and headed out the door towards the scud bunker when shots rang out.

I turned towards the Battery Commander, who was at the other end of the van. "That was gunfire!" My left hand pulled my 9mm pistol out of its holster and I held it at the ready. "I'll check it out!"[29]

I jumped to the ground and looked for backup. Someone was standing close by. "Who is that?" I asked.

"Doc."

"Got a weapon?"

"Yep."

"Then come with me."

We climbed to the next rise. I pulled out my 9mm magazine from a pocket in my promask case and inserted it in the pistol. I could hear no other shots, nor could I see any flashes from the high ground. A quick check at some of the bunkers gave us no clue as to where the shots had come from, although everyone agreed that they HAD heard shots.

I was talking to Staff Sergeant Kincaid when Lacher's voice came over the PA: "All personnel to the scud bunkers!"

A launch must be imminent, I thought to myself. Kincaid asked "Does that mean us?"

I did some calculations in my head: the Iraqis might or might not be getting ready to launch a scud missile; even if they DO launch it, it is unlikely that we are the target. Even if we are the target, it is unlikely that it would land within a mile of us.

On the other hand, we DEFINITELY heard shots. And if the Iraqis were going to launch commando raids on vital air defense sites, what better time to do so than when everyone is hiding from the scuds?

---

enemy, either directly or indirectly; shall suffer death or such other punishment as a court-martial or military commission may direct.

[29] Captain Fletchers later told me that the sight of me running out in the darkness with my pistol at "ready" was one of the scariest things he saw during the War. Like Sledge Hammer saying "Trust me, I know what I'm doing."

**EVERYTHING WAS NOT ALWAYS
AS IT SEEMED IN THE DESERT**

But they only launch commando raids in the movies. "Take your people to the bunker," I told Kincaid, then went to the J-box bunker with Doc in tow.

The soldiers at THAT bunker didn't know where the shots came from either. Suddenly Gonzales said "Hey, there's someone downrange!"

I looked at Launcher Three. In the darkness I could just barely make out figures moving there. "Status of the launchers?" I asked.

"Missiles armed, umbilicals connected, J-box in safe... for now. Last word we got, ADW is 'Yellow.'"

Gonzo climbed out of the bunker and headed for the launcher. "I'm going to check it out. If you hear shots, rock and roll, man!"

"You got it." One of the other soldiers replied.

"Nobody fires without permission," I amended. I got on the hand-held radio Doc had with him and managed to talk to the BC after some of the other key personnel got off of the net. "Sir, this is Crabtree. We have intruders in the downrange area."

"Who?"

"Don't know yet, Sir. Gonzales is investigating." I signed off, thinking great, shots to the left of us, intruders on our right, and the possibility of a missile coming down straight on our heads.

Gonzo was back a couple of minutes later. "They're from the unit next to us. They wanted to see what all the shooting was about."

"Did you tell them to get the Hell away from the missiles?" I asked. The last thing we needed was to "hold fire" because of unauthorized personnel downrange. Or to kill these guys when the Hawk missiles fired.

"Yeah!" And sure enough, the figures were moving away from the launcher.

SFC Mitchell was with us by then with a starscope, scanning the horizon for enemy commandos. "I love this shit."

"I could live without it." I muttered under my breath.

At that moment a soldier came over to me. "Sir, I know who fired the shots. It was an accident by one of our guys."

He gave me the name and I called up the CP on the hand-held radio. Captain Fletcher listened to my report and then said "Send the soldier and Sergeant Mitchell to the CP right away."

"Roger." I turned to Mitchell. "Did you get that?"

He gave a tired nod. He knew what was coming next would not be pleasant.

It turned out that one of the soldiers had loaded his rifle without permission. As if that wasn't bad enough, he had the weapon in "auto" instead of "safe" and was carrying it around that way. He was also carrying it with his

74

finger resting on the trigger, so when he tripped his finger reflex tightened on the trigger… and he shot up some sandbags.

We were very lucky no one got hurt. Captain Fletcher's normal composure went out the window and he got really mad. In fact, he made it clear how outraged he was that this soldier was irresponsible enough to endanger the rest of the unit.

We tightened up everything after that. We had everyone drop their empty magazines inspected weapons. Some of the magazines had rounds in them. In one case a grenade was loaded in a grenade launcher.

This was about the time I was on the road with SFC Tijerina and we were doing route reconnaissance. He noticed a place in a village we passed through that had what looked like a painting of a hamburger and maybe an American flag. So we stopped to check it out.

It was a very narrow restaurant with only one table. You ordered at the far end and beyond that was the kitchen. The proprietor spoke NO English, but eventually we got a couple of sodas and two hamburgers.

The meat had a strong taste to it. "This does NOT taste like beef." I told Tijerina.

Tijerina tried his. He turned to the owner. "Hey, is this beef?"

The owner simply looked confused and held up his hands.

"Beef!" Tijerina repeated. "You know: mooooooooo!"

NOW the guy perked up and shook his head. He then said "Baaaaaaah!"

We looked at each other. "Lamburgers?" Tijerina asked.

"I don't care," and proceeded to finish mine.

The momentum of events moved us forward, even as we lost some of our key people. Chief Lainey went to the rear for surgery and wound up being shipped home. Lt. Rich was sent back to the States due to family issues. Other units sent people back as well.

Rumors of a rotation policy were firmly squashed, to the relief of some and the consternation of others. Instead some effort was made to address recreation facilities in the theater. The Cunard Princess, an ocean liner, was leased by the Department of Defense so soldiers could cruise the Gulf in security and enjoy such things as the consumption of alcohol, bacon with breakfast and strolling the deck without a burqa (in the case of our female soldiers). Guests even had an opportunity to shop in the *suqs* of Bahrain.

**MAKING A RUN TO THE
LOCAL GENERAL STORE**

There was also the beach at Half-Moon Bay Recreation Center. This was an ad hoc facility but it provided soldiers an opportunity to get away from the 24-hour-a-day, 7-days-a-week routine of the desert. It had basketball courts, tennis, snorkeling, sailboats, water-skiing, etc. No cash bar,[30] though.

Bulgaria offered the Coalition the use of their Black Sea resorts as R&R facilities as well, but this offer was ignored, probably for logistical reasons. A few people were disappointed. That's pretty bad when former communist dictatorships look good to the troops in the field.

One or two soldiers from each company-sized unit were supposed to be sent to what facilities did exist. These soldiers were picked at random rather than on merit, as would normally be the case. In theory this would make it a trip ALL the soldiers would enjoy by empathy ("if everyone has a shot then everyone can imagine themselves there") but instead it just seemed to stir up a lot of petty jealousies.

Christmas was getting closer and closer. On the 22nd the battalion chaplain visited us. He brought his Bible, discreetly disguised as a dictionary as to not offend the locals. His improvised choir accompanied him as he said Mass for both our sites. The choir put a lot of love into their music and what they lacked in skill they made up for in enthusiasm. We all sang a special version of "The Twelve Days of Christmas (see next page)."

Everyone seemed to have a good time. It wasn't where we had imagined ourselves spending Christmas just five months before, but at least if we couldn't be with our families we could be with our unit.

Not long afterward I was given an official ORE test and passed, thanks to an excellent crew and NO GREMLINS this time. Our evaluator, Chief Couch, even mentioned how professional our run-through had been.

"I guess now it's LEGAL for me to shoot down aircraft!" I told my crew afterward. They all laughed and one said "Yeah, we were worried about that!"

Operating the system constantly in the desert with little in the way of distractions had honed our skills considerably. The experience I gained in Saudi Arabia was better than anything I could have gotten spending a year of normal training in the States.

It wasn't ALL work and drill at Radar Hill. After regular duty hours we frequently watched movies in the Big Top. "Robocop," "Tango and Cash," "Second Sight Detective Agency," "Full Metal Jacket," "Tucker," "The Running Man," and "House Party" were some of the films we watched. We also watched

---

[30] The penalty for running a cash bar in the Kingdom of Saudi Arabia is death.

On the First Day of Christmas, the Army gave to me...a foam rubber mattress for my cot!

On the Second Day of Christmas, the Army gave to me...two jungle boots!

On the Third Day of Christmas, the Army gave to me...three DCUs!

On the Fourth Day of Christmas, the Army gave to me....NO ammunition!

On the Fifth Day of Christmas, the Army gave to me....MY M-six-teen!

On the Sixth Day of Christmas, the Army gave to me...six magazines!

On the Seventh Day of Christmas, the Army gave to me...seven days of duty!

On the Eighth Day of Christmas, the Army gave to me...eight hours guard!

On the Ninth Day of Christmas, the Army gave to me...nine hundred sandbags!

On the Tenth Day of Christmas, the Army gave to me...ten-minutes warning!

On the Eleventh Day of Christmas, the Army gave to me...eleven MREs!

On the Twelfth Day of Christmas, the Army gave to me...twelve months in Saudi!

American TV shows on tape like "Star Trek, The Next Generation" and "Tales from the Darkside."

I tried to watch some of the tapes my Mom sent me. What I got was films of parades in the States. I know her heart was in the right place, but the last thing I wanted to see while stuck in Saudi Arabia was a bunch of floats.

On 24 December we prepared to go to a heightened state of readiness, just in case Saddam thought we would drop our guard around the holiday. The perimeter guard was increased and a "hot" crew kept on the system at all times.

Christmas 1990.

Again, our Mess Section put in a lot of time and energy to create a great Christmas spread. But where the mood during Thanksgiving was upbeat, Christmas was more somber. Sergeant First Class Yelle was not only an awesome cook but a God-fearing man. He led us in a prayer of thanks after we finished dinner.

The Big Top was decorated with a big, flat felt Christmas tree sent to us by the wives of our battery soldiers. It had an "ornament" for each soldier in the unit. The rest of the tent was decorated with items sent to "Any Soldier" and we watched some videos and enjoyed some of the "goodies" but the normal laughter and banter wasn't there. The holiday just reminded us how much we missed home.

We monitored another scud launch the day after Christmas. Saddam seemed to be playing a "war of nerves" with us, or trying to.

New Year's Eve 1990.

No party for us, just more of the same. While on shift in the control van the TD and the TCOs played "Headset Jeopardy" to make the time go faster, using a board version of the game at the battalion control van. The TD acted as the game show host, giving us categories such as "American History," "Geography," Science and Technology," and so on. We had no buzzers so you used your fire unit call sign to answer the question. Each fire unit was responsible for keeping track of which squares had been played while the battalion kept the score. A typical game might go like this:

"Once known as St. Petersburg," the TD began, "this city…"

"Bravo One!" I called out.

"Go, Bravo One."

"What is Leningrad?"

"Roger, 'what is Leningrad' is the correct answer for 300 points."

"Bravo One takes 'History' for 200."

One of the Radar Hill scud bunkers during an alert. This position was only partially dug out of a rock overhang but could provide some protection in the event of a scud strike, an ARM hitting a radar or a bombing run on the site itself. Note the radio to the right, tuned into AFN.

"He won at the Battle of Gettysburg but failed to follow up his victory against Robert E. Lee."

"Alpha Two!"

"Go, Alpha Two."

"Who was General Grant?"

"Negative."

"Charlie Two!"

"Go, Charlie Two."

"Who was General Meade?"

"Roger, 'Who was General Meade' was the correct answer for 200."

"Charlie Two takes 'Famous Authors' for 200..."

This kept everyone alert on the headset and broke the tedium of regular traffic over the net. Even the Radar Operators monitored and helped the TCOs with some of the questions. Sgt. Young would often help me with sports questions, which I could rarely answer. Young and I were doing pretty good New Year's Eve. But at the slightest sign of trouble the game would be forgotten and we would all be ready to track and destroy the enemy. We'd jump from Jeopardy to Missile Command pretty quick.[31]

No scud alerts, no missile launches. Midnight rolled around. The mechanical "battle clock" in each of our vans got down to the last couple of minutes of the year. Everyone on the headsets got quiet.

"Ten seconds." Someone said.

We all began to count down. "...eight ...seven... six... five... four... three... two... one... Happy New Year!"

We all exchanged greetings with one another. By now there had been personnel shifts, transfers, volunteers and replacements and we could hardly put a face against some of the voices we heard every day. Afterwards, no one really felt like playing the game anymore.

---

[31] During one game the question was something like "What was the War of Spanish Succession called in North America" and I answered "The French and Indian Wars" and I was sure I had the correct answer. The TD stated that the correct answer was Queen Anne's War. One of the few times the TD was right and I was wrong!

WE COULDN'T BE SURE HOW WELL
SADDAM'S AIRBORNE SENSOR
PLATFORM WORKED BUT WE
COULDN'T TAKE ANY CHANCES
EITHER

6. THE BIG JUMP

January 5th, 1991. It was the worst day yet.

December ended with cooler weather and in January we were starting to see very light rain, more of a drizzle. I was hobbling along the site when I saw the First Sergeant with a pair of binoculars watching the highway.

"What's going on?" I asked.

"Dunno. Looks like some kind of an accident."

Even without binoculars I could see the flashing lights of emergency vehicles in the distance. Then a medevac helicopter flew close to the hill, on its way to the scene. "Looks like they've got injuries, too," he added needlessly.

An hour later we found out the horrible truth: the accident involved one of our vehicles, the fuel tanker. It had been on the road and when it tried to turn to make the access road for Radar Hill it flipped over. The wet road was probably a factor.

Sergeant Davis got beat up pretty badly but because he was wearing his seat belt he avoided any life-threatening injuries. The driver was not so lucky.

Specialist James Brown, the same man who walked away from the scooploader accident when we arrived, was very badly hurt. He was airlifted to a Combat Support Hospital (CASH) and later would be sent to a fleet marine hospital pending airlift out of the theater. Brown was a good guy who didn't seem to have an enemy in the world. We all prayed for him or at least hoped for him to pull through.

The following day the BC held a morning formation to let everyone know what happened and to reemphasize safety. Brown's prognosis didn't look good. According to the information sent back down to us it was likely that he had a broken neck.

I got the thankless task of inventorying his things and packing them for shipment to his family. I felt angry but I couldn't put my finger on WHY. Maybe because it just didn't seem fair.

The battalion surgeon came by and I was given a "heads-up" that he was going to be checking on me. A couple weeks before I had sprained my ankle badly and I was also informed that if my foot was not properly healed that I would be sent to a rear-echelon job or maybe even back to the States. I don't recall if I actually had a DA3349 Physical Profile done on me, excusing me from running, jogging, marching, dancing, etc.

83

My foot was better but still painful. I didn't want to take any chances on being sidelined, though. Not this late in the game. I removed the tennis shoes I was authorized to wear and put on my boots. I walked, pain jabbing me every moment, to the missile area where the crewmen were doing their daily checks.

The medical officer showed up shortly afterwards. "How is everything going, Lieutenant Crabtree?"

"Just fine, Sir." I said as I ran my hand down the fuselage, feeling for scratches or anything else that might affect its performance.

"I heard your foot is bothering you…"

I was sweating like crazy from the pain. "Oh, it was bad at first but I'm fine now." I walked around the launcher, checking cable connections.

He watched me for a minute, then finally started heading back to the Admin area. I waited until he was out of sight, then slumped against the launcher. "Someone's going to have to help me. I don't think I can walk back to my tent!"

I probably set my recovery back but it was worth it. The battalion surgeon never sent me back to the rear.

Several of the NCOs and I passed the missile movement test a few days later. On shortwave we listened to Tariq Aziz's speech. As Saddam's Senior Stooge, he was now making it sound as if it was Israel's fault Iraq had invaded Kuwait.

The drizzle turned to rain. President Bush made a speech, announcing a January 16th deadline for Saddam to pull out of Kuwait. I heard it while in the control van and I said to the soldiers with me "If you ever wanted to know what an ultimatum sounded like, that's it."

Our terrorist threat level went up. Battalion notified us that it was possible that Saddam might launch a pre-emptive strike. It could consist of simultaneous attacks of scuds, chemical attacks, aircraft, terrorist attacks and commando raids, all coordinated and mutually supporting. In other words, scuds might be launched at our fighter airfields, making the pilots on the ground scramble for cover. Commandos might attack a vital Hawk missile unit to open a "gap" for fighter-bombers to exploit, who would then bomb the seaports with chemical weapons while terrorists attacked Saudi government targets… well, we clearly had to be on alert.

I wrote a couple of letters home. In my last package to my parents I sent film and three journals I had kept during Desert Shield. I wanted my parents to know what I was doing here in case anything happened to me.

RELIABILITY PROBLEMS

January 16th, 1991. The deadline passed with no response from Iraq and no attack by the Coalition. Everyone was kept in MOPP suits around the clock, protection against chemical attack (so long as you have the mask and gloves on too).

The HIPIR was broken and maintenance was working on it around the clock. Our fire platoon could not engage aircraft unless it used the Alpha system.

Unfortunately, the Alpha was proving to be somewhat less than satisfactory as a weapon system. It had a habit of picking up "ghost planes." I seem to recall at one point that we had a couple of MiG-23s listed on the engagement queue. This was very confusing... none of the Coalition partners flew MiG-23 fighter bombers in Saudi Arabia. The Iraqis had MiG-23s but unless they were attacking us and flying under the radar they should have been outside our range. Yet the system was telling me that they were there and good targets.

It was likely that the desert atmospherics were "spoofing" the system, fooling it into thinking an aircraft was much closer than it was. It was things like this that made us start to lose confidence in our "secret weapon."

2200. At the end of my shift I was told to report to the BC at the CP. When I got there all the officers and senior NCOs were there, waiting for Captain Fletcher. I figured this must be it.

The BC came in and we all snapped to attention. Fletcher told everyone to relax. "The moment we have waited for has arrived," he told us. "The war begins at 0300. It is no longer Desert Shield, it is Desert Storm. We will be moving out within the next two days. Any questions?"

No one stirred.

"Good luck." The BC concluded.

After almost two and a half months of sitting around in the desert it was almost a relief to finally get a combat mission. At least we would be DOING something.

During my next shift I watched for the vast Coalition Armada on the scope. I expected to see neat waves of attack aircraft but traffic only seemed a little heavier than normal. Meanwhile, the TD came on and had each fire unit confirm its wartime frequencies. We changed them to make it more difficult for the Iraqis to identify and locate us.

After being relieved by Wally I didn't think I would be able to sleep. I was wrong. I was out like a light.

When I woke up in our tent at 0600 I turned on the radio. A news program was discussing the first airstrikes so the fact that the war had started was no longer a secret. Later I tried AFN again and found out it was being jammed. Radio Baghdad was still broadcasting but that English-language "Voice

MUSIC IN THE DESERT

of Peace" crap was replaced by really indignant Arabic language content. I was surprised to find it was still on the air.

I grabbed my gear and headed to the PCP. Wally was manning the system. I took a look at the status board and asked "What's the matter with the HIPIR?"

Chief Dungy was also in the van and answered brusquely "Don't worry about it, we can use the HIPIR."

I walked out to the J-box to see how everyone was doing. The soldiers on duty there were ready and waiting for what everyone thought would be the inevitable counter-attack from the air. Off-duty soldiers were in the scud bunkers, wearing mop suits and keeping their rifles within reach and trying to get some sleep. AFN was coming in again and radios were playing: "... erican warplanes have struck targets all across Iraq and Kuwait, along with Saudi, British and Kuwaiti aircraft. Baghdad was struck this morning and anti-aircraft fire lit the sky. Apparently the fire was..."

Cruise missiles were sent into Iraq to wipe out the enemy's command and control network. Radars were being destroyed, leaving the Iraqis blind; aircraft followed up with strikes against Saddam's isolated air defense sites, taking them out one-by-one. Our opposite numbers were taking a beating as the air defense net that nominally protected Iraq was shredded with each strike, leaving gaping holes in the defense for further airstrikes.

The Iraqi air defenders were living our worst nightmare.

Meanwhile, the Hail Mary Move had begun. From our perch on Radar Hill we watched as what appeared to be one big column headed north: M1 tanks, artillery, support vehicles, supply trucks... hour after hour the column slowly headed north. In the meantime, our battalion would continue to provide the unseen "umbrella" of protection over them, ensuring the Iraqis couldn't hit them from the air when they were most vulnerable.

The aircraft within range at that moment were all "friendlies" of course. There was still no sign of the Iraqi Air Force, unless it had been obliterated already. That seemed highly unlikely as the IQAF had special bunkers to protect at least some of their planes.

Our pilots followed strict procedural guidelines, following altitude and speed limits. By following these rules (and making themselves very vulnerable to our missiles in the process) we minimized the need to send IFF signals out.

Or I should say MOST pilots followed these guidelines. A few came in at high speed and low altitude when returning to Saudi airspace. This would trigger a prompt from the Hawk computer and it would "order" an engagement. "Order" might be too strong of a word... when not set for Automatic

IN THE BUNKER

. Engagement the system could only "suggest." And if you pushed the button that was flashing the Automatic Data Processor would live up to its billing and automatically lock on to the aircraft and automatically fire at it with a missile that was now fully armed and integrated into the system. It would automatically destroy the aircraft, which is why we never let "Otto" run the system.

Instead, the TCO routinely overrode the computer, telling Otto to "ignore that one."

For Bravo the first day of the war was relatively uneventful. We manned the "front lines" of the ground-based air defense network but the enemy seemed extremely reluctant to challenge us for control of the air. Nothing happened those first shifts of the war.

But when it got dark the Iraqis began firing scuds again, only this time they meant business.

"SCUD LAUNCH! SCUD LAUNCH!" Joe's voice pierced the darkness. "ALL PERSONNEL TO THE BUNKERS!!!"

Wally and I were both off-shift and asleep in our tent, but not for long! It was 0300 the following day when we grabbed our gear and made for the CP as soldiers stumbled out of their tents and made for the bunkers below.

At the CP information was being relayed to us via the comnet. "Do you need me here or with Sean?" Wally asked.

"Go to the PCP!" Joe told him then went back to the radios. I made a run for the bunkers.

It was hard to find a spot in the packed space of the bunker. Soon, information was relayed to us from the CP: confirmed multiple launches. Target: Israel.

So this was Saddam's plan, to redefine the war. He hoped that by attacking Israel he could make this into a "Holy War against the Jews" instead of his invasion of another Muslim country. He hoped to split the Coalition, which contained several of his Arab neighbors. He hoped to become the good guy... at least in the Middle East.

At least it sounded as if the scud strikes were random and only using conventional warheads. On the radio we listened to some really stupid people standing out in the open in target areas to talk about being targeted. And this was when the media was introduced to the Patriot missile system.

The Army had talked weeks ago about Patriot and its (theoretical) ability to shoot down ballistic missiles. The Army talked about the need to defend against the scuds which would surely be loaded with chemical weapons, maybe even biological weapons. No one in the media paid much attention. Now it was

EVEN THOUGH THE PENTAGON WAS ATTEMPTING TO BE TRANSPARENT ABOUT OPERATIONS (WITHIN REASON) IT WAS CLEAR FROM SOME OF THE THINGS WE READ AND HEARD FROM JOURNALISTS THAT THEY JUST DIDN'T "GET IT."

doing the job and it seemed like it was all they could talk about. The media couldn't tell us enough about what a wonder weapon Patriot was.[32]

"Now Hawk HAS to shoot something down," said one of our soldiers. "Otherwise we'll never hear the end of this."

After several more strikes I was told to get the Blazer ready. By now we had a Saddam Hussein voodoo doll we got from the States tied to the front of the machine. This seemed like a good idea until we saw the amount of excitement this incited in Saudis manning checkpoints down the road.

We were getting ready for our own Big Jump. The scud launches continued into the daylight hours but we worked on getting the RSOP vehicle ready to go. At 1000 the BC got us together and briefed us on the situation.

The entire ground force of the Coalition was shifting. There would be three corps of ground forces which would form along their future jump-off points along the Iraqi and Kuwaiti borders.

The Marines and our Arab Allies would form the right wing of the line in a Coalition Corps, setting up on the Kuwaiti border facing the berm-and-trench network created by the Iraqis, the so-called Saddam Line. This was where the Iraqis expected us to attack and where they had dug battalion and regimental strong points throughout the desert. If the Iraqis expected the Marines and the Kuwaitis to move right through Kuwait then we would make sure their attention was fixed on Marines and Kuwaitis.

Meanwhile, VII Corps and its heavy armored units (including the UK's famous "Desert Rats") was relocating to the west of the Arab Allies, their right flank being anchored at the point where Kuwait, Iraq and Saudi Arabia border all met. Once the order was given and while the Iraqis continued to look to the south, VII Corps would smash into their flank and rear like a sledgehammer.

XVIII Airborne Corps was composed of the following divisions: 82nd Airborne ("the All Americans"), the 101st Air Assault ("Screaming Eagles"), the 24th Mechanized Infantry ("Victory") and the French 6th Light Armored ("Daguet"). This force would be to the left of VII Corp and once the order was given would move north to the Euphrates River, cutting off the Iraqi concentration of forces in southern Iraq.

With the air campaign fully underway the Iraqis were "blind," that is they had no means of air reconnaissance to see what was going on the Saudi border. Electronic restrictions would prevent them from using signal intelligence to figure out who was where and aggressive raiding into Iraqi

---

[32] Of course, we were also subjected to such Pulitzer-winning reporting as "the use of Patriot infra-red missiles" and "the U.S. hasn't done any training in the desert warfare since WWII."

territory would discourage them from getting too curious as to what was going on across the border.

"Our own part in this has been moved ahead of schedule," Captain Fletcher told us. "The RSOP teams will have to move out immediately in order to link up with a Brigade PADS team at King Khalid Military City. It will then proceed to the far west of the new line, only 20 kilometers from the Iraqi border. That's where our new sites will be." He showed us on his map: the trip would involve traveling at least 750 kilometers. "Task Force Scorpion will be defending XVIII Airborne Corps. Our battery sector will be over the French 6th Division."

The plan was to establish three "cells" along the new line. Each cell would be composed of two Hawk fire units (the fire platoons of a regular Hawk battery) and a single Patriot fire unit (one battery).The Patriot unit would provide TBM protection for specific potential targets (in our case, the small airfield of Rafha) and we would protect the Patriots with 360 degree coverage.

"The battery will stand down from its air defense mission at 1200 today and then secure for movement. The rest of the battery will move out on MSR Mercedes at 1645 tomorrow." Fletcher looked us in the eyes. "Any questions?"

"Yes, Sir. Where's my map?"

He rapidly stashed away the military map he had been using to brief us. "We don't have any. You'll have to get one at KKMC. When can you be ready to go?"

"Sir, Tijerina has the vehicle fueled and ready. All we need to do is throw some personal gear on and we can roll out within 30 minutes."

"Good." And then the BC left to attend other matters.

Being placed in charge of the RSOP team for this critical move was no small matter, at least not to me. I was determined to succeed.

Ron and Phil drove up to Radar Hill from the 2nd Fire Platoon and Phil threw his gear in my vehicle. Once again, it would be a "non-standard" operation. It would be me, Phil and Sergeant First Class Tijerina on this trip. We had a tourist map to find KKMC (which wasn't on it), had Saddam Hussein tied to the front bumper and were flying a small guidon with the number 13. What could go wrong?

It was good to be on the road and DOING something. Morale was high among the air defenders as we left… I think all the inactivity might have had a role in the blues everyone was feeling over the last few weeks. Just traveling the route and getting away from the constant scud alerts coming through the air defense net was already bringing up MY morale.

Traffic was bad but tolerable on our first leg, returning to an-Nariyah. But once there it was practically bumper-to-bumper along Tapline Road, known as MSR Dodge for Army planning purposes. Fortunately a HEMMT let us squeeze into traffic.

We weren't WATCHING the long strand of vehicles headed to the new corps areas, now we were IN it. Miles ahead of us and miles behind us, nothing but tracks and other Army vehicles. We were headed west now, every once in a while a vehicle would be headed East. We almost had to swerve off the road as now-empty British tank transporters headed to the rear, taking up more of the road than was fair.

Cargo helicopters also headed west, flying parallel to the Tapline Road, some of them with sling loads for new camps which were not built yet. Attack helicopters flew just to the north of the road, screening our movement from the Iraqis.

Traffic slowly thinned as we made progress. I checked the map, and based on what I had seen on the BC's military map I thought I knew where to find KKMC. Eventually we reached Hafar al-Batin and headed south. It was just getting dark when we saw a sign for King Khalid Military City and followed it until we saw what had to be the Air Defense Compound: there was a huge monument composed of a Hawk missile crossed with the barrel of an antiaircraft gun mounted on a stone pedestal (now THAT'S class!). We arrived at our destination without getting lost or delayed.

The Air Defense Compound was the home of that 11th ADA Brigade Tactical Operation Center (TOC). This placed the TOC in a much more centralized position to control the air defense network. Meantime, the 11th ADA Brigade Command Post, providing the administrative and staff support for the ADA units was back in Dhahran in the "Ice Palace."

An NCO met us when we pulled in. "If you want the PADS team you'll have to go to the TOC. If you want to eat you'll have to go to the mess hall right away, they're getting ready to close."

We had time so we got something to eat. The food was marginally better than what we were used to at our site. Afterwards Tijerina arranged for a couple of cots for us to sleep on with First Sergeant Lippincot, the HHB top sergeant. He gave us a quick brief on the layout of the site and where the scud bunkers were but my mind was wandering. I'd pay the hard way for not paying attention later on that night.

We drove to the TOC, which was deeper within the compound. The building was surrounded by very high berms and looked like a fortress in the dark. We had to make a sharp right-angle to get inside the perimeter. Once

Practicing site layout with the M2 Aiming Circle. The M2 was vital for establishing each piece of equipment's location relevent to each other as well as the site location. However, conditions in Saudi Arabia made it impossible to establish location with certainty.

The downrange area of radar Hill. This area was kept clear most of the time as it would be extremely unhealthy to be near the "birds" when they were launched.

there, we couldn't find a human-sized door until we came across a guard who was keeping out the riff-raff.

Once inside the big building we made our way to where the 11th ADA Brigade TOC was located. Command and Control vehicles were parked inside, along with communication vans. Computers were everywhere, tracking command and control data. The operators were relaying information, talking to units, providing guidance.

While we waited to speak to someone about the PADS team the brigade commander, Colonel Skip Garrett, came into the room to check on some information, looked Phil and me over for a moment, and then left. As the top air defender in the theater I guess they were keeping him pretty busy; his Patriot units were the only defense from Saddam's scud missiles.

The things might be junk, but it turned out they were UNSTOPPABLE junk. Or almost, anyway.

An S-3 major finally showed up to give us a situation brief. "OK, show me your map."

"Sir, I wasn't given a map. I was hoping YOU had one."

This visibly irritated him. "Well, give me your coordinates."

I felt that cold chill I always get when I suddenly realize I've made a mistake. "Uh, I left my book in the vehicle…."

"WHAT?" He was visibly angry as he pointed to a nearby wall map. "You're going up to the Iraqi border and you don't have a map, you don't know the challenge and password, and you don't have the coordinates for your sites?! You're liable to get lit up by our own people!"

I did in fact know the challenge and password, I had the coordinates in the vehicle and as for the map, well I didn't see how it was my fault that there were not enough maps to go around. But I was a lowly 2nd lieutenant and he was a major and as unfair as it seemed right was on the side of the oak leaves.

"Get your heads out of your asses!" The major explained. I felt bad for Lt. Riley… even if this guy was right about me (which he wasn't) he had no reason to believe Phil was an idiot too. But maybe he just had to get it out of his system. With all the scud launches and the constant calls the S-3 section probably was running on no sleep.

"Look, I don't want you guys to get killed." The major continued. "I like you. I don't KNOW you, but I LIKE you."

I think I preferred getting yelled at.

We found the PADS team nearby. The NCOIC, Staff Sergeant Tanis, handed over what looked like a medium-sized, gray transistor radio.

"What the Hell is this?" I asked him.

"It's the commercial navigator." He replied.

I took another look at the device. "How does it work?"

"You mean you don't know?"

"I've never seen anything like this before."

Putting our heads together we came to the conclusion that without reliable military maps to verify our site locations (or even find them!) or training on the new device we would have to use the GPS receiver that the PADS team was equipped with. The PAD team would depart the next morning with all the battery RSOP teams in tow and locate each site one at a time. Once Task Force Scorpion was finished the PADS team would return to KKMC.

"Scud alert," one of the operators said from a nearby van. "Weather radar coming up."[33]

There were a couple of tense minutes while the staff officers debated whether or not to send another general alert over the air defense net. Before a firm decision was reached the same person announced "Radar shutdown."

One of the nearby officers, clearly relieved, said "They do this all the time. I think they're wising up to the fact that we can detect them."

I found a commo soldier. "Send a message to our battalion headquarters and have them relay it to our battery: 'RSOP team arrived at KKMC. Prepared to leave for sites by 0600 tomorrow and arrive near Rafha by 1800. Foresee no problems.'"

He nodded and I figured I had done everything I could do. We drove back to HHB to get some sleep before what was bound to be a very busy day. While we were getting out our sleeping bags a large puppy came over to see us.

"Hey boy!" Tijerina patted him. He turned to one of the Brigade soldiers, "What's his name?"

"Scud." Someone answered.

"What a name for a dog," I said, trying to get comfortable on the cot.

"Hey, you're taking off your boots?" Phil asked.

"I can't sleep with shoes on." I said, putting them under the cot.

"What if there's a raid?"

"Then I'll get them on again, real quick."

We settled down for the night. It wasn't long before air raid sirens began to wail, and these weren't the improvised ones we had been using at Radar Hill: these were the real thing! Somewhere, someone yelled "SCUD LAUNCH!"

---

[33] Possibly an RMS-1 "End Tray" associated with the scud missile system.

Tijerina, Riley and I all threw open our sleeping bags as occupants of the building scrambled to get the heck out of there. It was remarkably empty by the time I got one of my boots on.

"Come on, Sir!" TJ Told me.

"Go ahead! I'll be there in a second!" I told him as I struggled with the other damned boot. It finally slipped on and I grabbed my rifle and my mask without thinking about it. I stumbled into the darkness outside the building.

The drone of sirens (it sounded like dozens of them) were coming in loud and clear from King Khalid Military City, even though we were miles outside the main base. I looked around but there wasn't another soul in sight; everyone else must have already been in shelters.

I felt fear. There has always been something about air raid sirens that bothers me when I hear them, whether it was during a movie on TV or the monthly Civil Defense test. Only this wasn't a test and it wasn't a film.

Then the lights went out. Why the Hell did they turn out the damn lights?! Is a blackout supposed to save us from scud missiles? Even if I could remember where they first sergeant said the bunker was I wouldn't be able to find it. I could imagine a scud screaming down from space to the very spot I was standing on... and for some reason I had this strange, unreasoning fear that the Army would tell my parents that I died as a hero or something when I actually died because I didn't pay attention to instructions.

Then the sirens started winding down. And the lights came back on. And people started appearing out of nowhere. Someone yelled "All clear!" The missiles hadn't been aimed at us at all.

We went from fear to exhilaration in nothing flat.

7. BORDERLINE

Desert Storm was barely three days old and we were making our second big jump. Our little convoy of CUCVs included the PADS team and the RSOP teams from the other batteries setting up in our sector. We headed west from Hafar al-Batin, getting closer to the Iraqi border all the time. The route we were on, called "MSR Dodge" on Army maps but just Tapline Road to everyone else, would become notorious for motor vehicle accidents over the next few weeks but that day our trip was fairly uneventful. We had to weave in and out of traffic, passing some of the French, but after a couple hours we found that we practically had the road to ourselves.

Eventually we drove through the ceremonial gates of Rafha. Every large Saudi town seemed to have these. In Rafha's case it consisted of three small towers, which looked like rooks, connected by wooden arches. The town itself was a set of one- and two-story buildings. We pulled over in the parking lot of a hotel. I don't recall the name but it sure wasn't the Rafha Hilton.

We climbed out of the vehicles and stretched. Staff Sergeant Tanis got out the "Slugger," the GPS receiver used by Patriot for determining precise location, and we all gathered around the device to make sure it was working prior to moving to our new missile sites.

This was all a learning experience for me. Hawk units didn't rate GPS, which was still new at the time. What we were expected to do was use an M2 aiming circle to determine the base location by triangulation on a map. In other words, we basically used surveying equipment to check the azimuth of two landmarks on the map, reverse their azimuths, draw a line from each on the new number and where the lines cross is you location.

But in the Arabian Desert there aren't a lot of large radio towers, mountain peaks and skyscrapers to "shoot" with the M2. Oh, and we didn't have a map anyway.

This made GPS the greatest invention since the bazooka. Once we were satisfied that we had the Slugger[34] working right we headed out, using the gadget to guide us to the Bravo One pre-planned position. In cases like this we were given coordinates as to where to set up our weapon systems. Staff officers at battalion provided these based on guidance from brigade and using maps

---

[34] From SLGR, or "Small Lightweight GPS Receiver."

Lt. Riley and Staff Sgt. Tanis try to get a fix with the GPS at Rafah.
When we arrived at the town there was virtually no Coalition
presence but that would change quickly, given the airfield nearby.
Our unit protected the area from air attack for the next few weeks.

100

and staff tools. But traditionally the RSOP team on the ground had some leeway based on the local geography and other factors.

We moved south of the Tapline Road. We passed near the town dump, which appeared to simply be a spot out in the desert where everyone agreed to toss their garbage. It smelled, especially in spots where fires had been lit, and made us wonder why no one tried to organize a landfill.

We followed the azimuth and watched as the range counted down to the spot where we would establish the missile site. "Just a little farther," Tanis told us, staring at the readout. 2,000 meters, 1,500 meters, 500 meters... "Just a little bit... this should be it."

And there in front of us was a wide-eyed Arab family surrounded by their flock of sheep.

Tijerina laughed. "Hey Sir, this is YOUR land now. Tell 'em they're evicted."

Of course, none of them spoke English but when we made it clear with hand gestures (and speaking very loudly) that they had to go they shooed their sheep off. Tanis took readings off the Slugger, the ones we would need for the PCP's computer when it arrived and we marked the "base" for the system. We started putting up the signs and stakes.

An MP vehicle pulled up, the first Americans we had seen since we arrived at Rafha.

"Who are you guys?" the driver asked.

"Bravo 2-1 ADA," Riley answered.

"Air Defense Artillery?" the MP asked, a little excited. "Patriot?"

"No, Hawk."

"Oh." The soldier was clearly disappointed that one of those high-tech Patriots would not be protecting the corner of the desert he happened to be sitting in.

"Yeah, but there'll be a Patriot battery nearby as part of the local defense." I added.

At that the driver perked up. "Patriot!" He gave us a "thumbs up." "All right!"

As the MP drove off Tijerina said "Sir, we have GOT to shoot something down."

We did the second site next. Actually, we did it TWICE. Riley decided there was some slightly higher ground nearby. Well, it was Riley's call as he was the one who was ultimately responsible, and we seemed to have enough time to do it. There was just the three of us to get it all done and it was well into the night by the time we had everything ready. We moved to Tapline Road to wait for the arrival of the convoy.

PATRIOTS
ENGAGE!

We woke up to the sound of a Blackhawk helicopter flying along the road. We tried to get ourselves cleaned up and shaved. Sergeant Tijerina heated up some water for coffee by burning a deodorant stick, a method that worked surprisingly well. And to be honest, we weren't going to miss it; TJ's deodorant was fighting a losing battle against the desert.

A few Army vehicles began to appear on the road. Some would even stop and ask for directions or other information we didn't have. "Sorry, Sir. We just got here ourselves," I told one captain.

An MP HMMWV with an all-female crew drove by and waved at us. Everyone grinned like it was a day at the beach. A really BIG beach.

I noted a small pickup that passed us going down the road, headed east. I could see three Arabs in the rear window but thought nothing of it.

"Did you see that?" Tijerina asked.

"See what?" I said as I continued to shave.

"Those Arabs." He said, looking in the direction they had disappeared. "They had an AK-47 and were arguing."

I continued to scrape my skin with my disposable razor. "Sure they were."

"No, really. They were arguing about who would get the rifle. I don't think they even saw us."

It was too early to deal with another one of Tijerina's tall tales. "Let me see the radio."

We tried to pick up the news the day before but the only English-language station we could find was Radio Netherlands. I tuned the thing until I got some music. British and American, but that didn't necessarily mean anything in this part of the world.

"What station is that?" Riley asked.

"I don't know. We'll have to wait and find out."

The music ended and a female voice came on. "This is the English-language service of Radio Moscow. And now for the news..."

Glasnost or no glasnost, Radio Moscow wouldn't normally be considered a reliable source of information, but it was all we could get.

Mainly the news focused on the ongoing problems in the different Soviet republics. The problem was mostly one of NOT wanting to be Soviet republics anymore. They also spoke about the ongoing air campaign over Iraq and the latest scud strikes. Despite intercepts by Patriot the enemy's missiles were still doing damage and were now claiming lives.

"We now return to our music programme," the female announcer said in her BBC English voice. But the guy who came on next did NOT sound like he was on BBC. Or Radio Moscow, for that matter:

**TRIANGULATION
SHOT**

"HEY, this is Sergei Androvovitch and you're tuned to our Rock and Roll Hour! My first dedication goes out to Mikhail Deorandov down in the Georgian Republic, who wants to hear some Beatles! So…"

"This must be some kind of a joke," I said.

"It can't be real," said Riley.

"… for Mikhail, here's 'Back in the USSR!'"

As the Beatles tune played I heard Tijerina say "All right! Radio Moscow."

The DJ sounded like someone you would tune in to on a Cincinnati rock station, not someone who graduated the Reed Smith Academy of International Broadcasting, located in beautiful downtown Pinsk. The most entertaining part of the broadcast was when Sergei Androvovitch came back on the air and talked about a Canadian letter he got from a long-time listener of Radio Moscow: "'Dear Radio Moscow; I have been a devoted listener for many years now and enjoy the alternative music and viewpoints your station provides.'"

I imagined some pretentious professor with a beard, taking a break from teaching his classes and sitting in his cottage facing a gothic tower on campus and smoking a pipe. A photo of Lenin is on one side of the window and Marx on the other.

"'However,'" the DJ continued to read, "'I must protest this recent change in your station's format. The clearly-Americanized DJ playing decadent Rock and Roll music is the sort of thing one can find anywhere on the AM and FM bands.'"

Now I imagined the same guy turning off his radio, pushing aside the latest copy of Soviet Life, and writing an impassioned letter: What station could he now listen to when he wants to listen to Shostakovich's Greatest Hits or Strelnikov reading highlights from Pravda?

"'Please STOP playing this bourgeois music or I will have to cease listening to Radio Moscow. Signed, Carl Morton in Alberta.'"

My imaginary communist sympathizer signs the letter with a flourish, then stops and considers whether he should add a postscript accusing the DJ of being a Trotskyite. Nah, that might be a bit much. He seals the envelope and takes it out to the post.

"Well," said Sergei, "I guess it's 'Goodbye Carl, hello Sting!'"

We all looked at each other. "I guess the Cold War really IS over." I said.

Later a HMMWV from the 82nd Airborne Division pulled up and asked if we knew where the divisional artillery was supposed to set up. Once again I had to apologize.

The major started to drive off, then seemed to have second thoughts. "Has anyone briefed you on the local situation here?"

"No, Sir."

He gestured to the west, in the direction of Rafha. "THAT village is pro-Saudi." He then pointed down the road to the east. "THAT village down there is pro-Iraqi. Don't be caught in THAT village after dark."

"'Stay out of the local village after dark.'" I said back to him. "Right, Sir."

"Oh and the local Emir or Chief or whatever went ahead and opened the armory at Rafha and started handing out weapons." His HMMWV pulled away. "Be careful!" He yelled back at us.

I thought about the three Arabs in the pickup truck. I turned. Sergeant First Class Tijerina didn't say anything, he just smiled an "I-told-you-so" smile.

At about 1000 hours a lone Stinger vehicle pulled up with the BC. "The rest of the convoy is about 40 minutes away," he told me as he got out of the vehicle. He looked a little haggard, but otherwise was ready to go despite the long trip.

I briefed him on the locations of the two sites and the local conditions. He told me that, surprisingly, we had only suffered one vehicle breakdown during the long road march and had to leave a generator down the road.

Phil returned from a last-minute check of the AFP II site and used binoculars to try to spot it from the road. Soon the rest of Bravo Battery arrived: battered and loaded down it reminded me of pictures I had seen of gypsy caravans. Weary as everyone was there was a sense of urgency to get to the sites and get the "umbrellas" up over the extreme left flank of the line.

Tijerina and I led the vehicles to their positions at the AFP-I site. Whitmire and Fletcher tweaked some of the locations but we got everything up and running. The soldiers, exhausted from their 600-mile+ trip, fell asleep on the equipment.

The next morning we woke everyone and did "stand-to," assuming a defensive posture around the site. Captain Fletcher got everyone started on digging foxholes. This was hard work but we did it and assigned fighting positions to everyone. At less than 20 kilometers away, we were now within artillery range of the Iraqis. All they needed was someone spotting for them.

And wouldn't you know it, they HAD artillery spotters… the media. One or two idiot reporters during the Big Jump revealed that they were with U.S. . Army units moving "near Hafir al-Batin" or "on the Tapline Road" or "near Rafha." Thanks, CNN, for making life more interesting for us! It's not like the Iraqis actually have maps of this area or anything.

More units moved into the area, now that the umbrella was up. With just the one road it would take a while to get everything into place. In the meantime we worried that the Iraqis might suddenly send a regiment or brigade

SIGHTS ALONG TAPLINE ROAD

from the two divisions spotted across the border and seize Rafha, cutting off the northwest part of Saudi Arabia from the eastern region. There wasn't much we could do to stop them at the time, although we didn't doubt we'd give them a bloody nose when the 82nd retook it.

The Iraqis, however, seemed content to just "wait and see" on their side of the border.

Aside from the flies which started showing up at the Rafha Site (even the vermin, it seemed, hated the town dump and were looking for a new place to hang out) we had issues with Arabs trying to drive through the missile site, some at high speed. One almost ran into a loaded launcher. However, after one particularly enterprising local picked his way between bunkers and around concertina wire and drove at high speed through the admin area. "Stop that vehicle!" I yelled.

Several soldiers were in the immediate area. One walked into the path of the little pickup and carefully aimed his M16 rifle at the driver...

The driver skidded to a stop. An NCO gestured to the man in a big arc and the Arab nodded in understanding: GO AROUND. We had few intrusions after that. Word must have circulated.

Because there were so many different types of vehicles in the Coalition, including a few that had also been sold to the Iraqis, instructions were sent down to add a recognition emblem on all machines. An upside-down "V" was painted on the sides of tanks, trucks, and armored vehicles in an effort to minimize possible fratricide.

We tried to get caught up on the news. Now that the Air War had begun Iraq was being pounded daily. We could see contrails of aircraft flying from the west, then making a "left" into Iraqi airspace. Apparently Rafha was an aid to navigation.

Stories were also coming out about pilots who were captured by the Iraqis. Some made statements on TV about how the U.S. "wrongly attacked the peaceful people of Iraq." These statements would have been more convincing had they not been made by men who had clearly been beaten before-hand.

If Saddam thought that this would demoralize us, he was mistaken.

Bravo Battery was so close to the border that the Air War could be seen every night on my scope as friendly aircraft conducted missions over Iraqi airspace and the few hostiles Iraq was able to get airborne tried to avoid being shot down. Then, on January 22nd, one of the hostiles suddenly turned south, towards Saudi Arabia. It was now a potential threat not just to Coalition forces in the area but also to Rafha, the nearby airfield and... us.

I hit the siren and went to "Blazing Skies." I gave the crewmen their instructions and we prepped the system for an engagement. Meantime, I tried to establish contact with the TD, which had assumed control of our sector by then: "One-Six? One-Six? I have a designated hostile approaching. One-Six?"

There was no response. The voicelink always seemed to fail at critical moments and it was worse at this new site. I turned to the commo guy and told him "Check the link and find out what's going on!"

"Downrange clear. Launchers standing by," I heard over the headset. I acknowledged and turned in my chair as the BC entered.

"What's going on?" he demanded, looking at the console. I pointed to the hostile, which was now within missile range. "What does the TD say?"

"I get no answer, Sir." And I tried to raise them again. Even though the target was a Confirmed Hostile we were under very restrictive rules of engagement: the aircraft would have to carry out a "hostile act" before we could fire at it, such as dropping paratroopers or bombs. Now how the Hell am I supposed to find out if an airplane 30 kilometers away is dropping paratroopers or bombs?

There were only two exceptions to this restriction: if it entered an invisible "self-defense zone" around the battery or if the TD gave specific permission to engage that track. Such permission was not forthcoming. By the time voice contact was reestablished the aircraft was back at its base, oblivious to its potential destruction.

Word got around to the soldiers manning the rest of the Hawk system that Bravo One had an opportunity to shoot but didn't. Competition amongst the fire units was intense, and everyone wanted to be the first one to shoot down an Iraqi plane.

Aside from the Rules of Engagement and the fact that we didn't have contact with the TD, I had no idea who had designated the aircraft a "hostile." It's possible that it was just a probable based on some criteria, like violating an airspace procedure. On the other hand, it might have been another Iraqi attempt to do "reconnaissance by fire," trying to get us to bring up our radars, revealing our position, then diving for the desert floor before we can get missiles ready.

Even if we destroyed the aircraft (ESPECIALLY if we destroyed the aircraft!) it would have confirmed to the Iraqis that there must be something out here worth defending. So we stayed silent, maintaining emissions control to keep Saddam guessing.

It was about this time that we got word that Brown had died while being flown to Italy for further treatment. So much had happened since the accident that it seemed like a year since we last saw him, but it had only been a

HOLY LAND IMPACTS

couple of weeks. With the loss of Specialist Brown everyone in the battery was pretty down; his death affected all of us to some degree or another and perhaps for different reasons. While he was a friend to many his death made us all conscious of the fact that we would soon be crossing the border into the enemy's defenses.

Would there be mines? Would Saddam use gas? Would he try to take us out first with scuds or wild weasels? It was best not to dwell on these things.

Fortunately, the pace was picking up fast. Rafha's airfield was being used to airlift troops into our sector and there were a constant stream of C-130s overhead and in a distant traffic pattern, which we watched on the scope. Initially it was the 101st and 82nd Airborne Divisions but later the French would bring in part of the 6th Light Infantry Division via the airfield as well.

I thought it was interesting that both myself at Rafha Site and some air traffic controller at the airfield were both watching the pattern, but for different reasons. He was making sure they flew safely and made it in and out with no mistakes. I was keeping an eye out for anything that didn't belong in the pattern... it would only take one wolf among the sheep to cause chaos on this end of the line.

But this was unlikely thanks to the AWACS which was running its pattern along the border. AWACS are truly technological wonders, detecting and tracking aircraft at long range, providing guidance to fighters to intercept enemy planes and doing electronic surveillance of the environment. AWACS was another data resource for the TD, helping us to make the right engagements.

The same night we got news of Brown's death Captain Fletcher waited in the van during my night shift. There was a running joke that I was jinxed somehow;[35] every time an Iraqi aircraft popped up it always seemed to be during my shift. Captain Fletcher wanted to be close by in case another hostile came within Hawk range during the night, but he gave up at about 2330 hours.

Ten minutes after he departed the exact same situation popped up: one of the hostiles made a turn and came within range. I checked with the downrange personnel and confirmed we were clear. I then called for Captain Fletcher to return to the van. He was as eager as I was to get a shot in, and this time our voicelink was working. "One-Six? This is Bravo-One. I have a target and request permission to engage."

"Show me the target, Bravo-One." I heard over the headset. I sent a pointer on the scope, which was relayed via the datalink to the ICC where the Tactical Director was sitting way down the line.

---

[35] Actually, I'm just unlucky to some.

There were several minutes of waiting while Sergeant Young, the BC and I watched and discussed the target. It was a single aircraft and didn't seem to be in a particular hurry despite all the air activity going on that night. If it was an attempt to spoof us into giving away our position by fire it was a suicidal one.

"Bravo One, One-Six," The TD finally came back on, "there are too many friendlies in that area."

I sensed my opportunity slipping. "Roger, I see them, but I can bring down the target without endangering…"

"Negative, Bravo One."

I took my headset off in disgust. "I forgot that the Air Force is supposed to get all the glory."

Captain Fletcher was like the rest of us, looking for a chance to take a shot at the enemy, but at the time we thought we could afford to be patient. We were convinced that sooner or later the Iraqi Air Force would have to leave their hiding places and their bunkers and come out to fight. Little did we know that they WOULD come out but they had something other than fighting in mind.

The "news" started to filter in over the headset in the form of information exchanged between the TD and the TCOs. "Intel reports that only small numbers of Iraqi aircraft are being destroyed in air-to-air combat and in bombing attacks on enemy airfields." The TD told us.

"They must be saving them for the Ground War," one of the TCOs replied. "They'll want to give their troops close air support."

"Fine," said another TCO. "That means we'll get a shot at them."

"We've deployed a Patriot task force from Germany to Israel." The TD said. Israel was still getting hammered by Iraqi scuds as Saddam did his best to provoke Israel into retaliating against him and make his lie about this being a "Holy War against the Jews" true.

8. F-16 INCIDENT

On January 24th I was given another road mission, this time to go to battalion headquarters for a class conducted by Staff Sergeant Tanis on the use of the Voyager, a new civilian-model GPS device. SFC Tijerina drove and Doc hitched a ride so he could pick up medical supplies.

I understood that these trips were part of my job, but they could also be frustrating. I felt like my focus wasn't being kept on the task at hand: shooting down Iraqi aircraft. Shooting them down often and loudly until there weren't any left.

The new headquarters site was 50 miles east on Tapline Road. The road was no longer empty of traffic, as it had been when the RSOP team drove through. We spent considerable time dodging U.S. Army trucks and French armored cars. We passed Logbase Charlie, a huge supply depot covering much of the north side of Tapline Road... it simply hadn't been there before. The key XVIII Airborne Corps facility had acres and acres of material: bottled water, MREs, spare parts, ammunition, you name it. Charlie One hawk site was nearby, protecting this vital asset from surprise air attack.

Turning south we proceeded to the battalion site, a compound ringed with defensive positions. We gave the password, gained access and parked at the aid station. I walked from there to the S-3 Operations area. I ran into Captain Belleperche, who told me "The class it at 1300. At YOUR site."

Another day of garbled communications, obviously. Oh well. I decided to go by the mail section while we were there. There was no letter mail but lots of boxes. We started loading up when the First Sergeant showed up on his own run. We departed in B103, leaving him to take the rest.

I couldn't help noticing before we left the number of soldiers walking around clutching brand-new desert boots, still tied together with their laces. I made a mental note to let our supply sergeant know when I got back.[36]

The ride was almost fun. I got a box from my Mom and Dad and shared brownies with everyone. Doc leafed through some wrestling magazines from one of TJ's boxes and we all looked through newspapers and magazines.

Back at the site I left Tijerina to hand out boxes. I went to the PCP and got there just in time for my shift.

---

[36] It was a waste of time to notify anyone. The new sand-colored boots rarely made it down to battery level, where work conditions in the sand had a tendency to wear out the boots we had arrived with.

The shift was quiet until it was about halfway over. Then one of Charlie Battery's fire units came on the headset. "Zero-One, I have a possible hostile track."

I looked at the screen and saw the target. But the TD came on and said "Just ignore him." I went back to looking through my mail.

A minute later the controller changed his mind. "Charlie-Two, engage designated track. It is a confirmed hostile."

"Damn!" I turned to the scope and watched closely. Sergeant Young, sitting on the Radar Operator's console looked at me quizzically. He could not hear the conversation between the TCOs and the TD.

"The TD has just given Charlie permission to engage a track!" I told him, I thought I recognized the track in question, a "diamond" (hostile) symbol moving near the Charlie sub-sector.

Young turned back to his controls. "All right!"

The target in question was some distance away from our Hawk site, although I could "see" it on the long-range scope. I listened for the message "Missile Away!" which would let us all know that a Hawk had been fired but no such message came. Instead, Charlie told the TD they could not engage.

"Charlie says they can't shoot," I told Young. "The TD is switching to Alpha."

The Alpha TCO, who was sitting closest to the track, was reluctant. "Target is above operational altitude."

My forehead furrowed. Well, the TD can see your data so he already knows that. And sure enough, the TD responded "Roger, engage the target."

"Speed is also too low."

"UNDERSTOOD." The TD said. "Engage."

I turned to Young. "I don't believe this! The TCO won't shoot!"

"Ask the TD to give US the target!"

I looked at the scope and shook my head. It was too far out from our location.

After a minute of silence the TD came back on: "Target will be hard to acquire. It is now out-bound."

The frustration was obvious in his voice: "Understood. Try ANYWAY."

By this time I couldn't stay in my seat any longer. "What is WITH them?! " Even though we all wanted to be first it was maddening to be sitting here and watching not one but two fire units pass on the opportunity.

"Unable to get a lock," said the Alpha TD.

"Roger! Charlie-Two, engage the target."

"They've switched back to Charlie Battery," I told Young.

"Uh, Zero-One, this is Charlie-Two. HIPIR is non-op."

By this time I was watching the scope and doing calculations in my head as to whether a Hawk fired from my position could reach the target. True, it was at extreme range, but it seemed to be disinclined to maneuver. The missile MIGHT get it before its open-ended hydraulic system[37] stopped working. But I knew it was all academic anyway: the TD would never give me permission to engage when there were other fire units closer to the target.

There was a lot of pressure to be the first one to destroy an enemy aircraft with a Hawk missile. In fact, there was a rumor that Raytheon, the company which made the system, had a bottle of illicit champagne[38] stashed for the crew which brought down a warplane. Of course, there was also a lot of pressure not to make a mistake...

We watched helplessly as the target turned north for home, oblivious of our efforts to destroy it.

I handed my headset over to Sergeant Young and went to the field phone in the back of the van. I gave the CP an update on what was going on, no doubt embellishing it out of frustration. Then Young yelled "More hostiles coming in!"

"Got to go! I told Lacher and slammed the phone down.

"At least seven in-bound targets," I heard the TD say. "160 kilometers and closing."

I hit the siren. Blazing Skies once again (or would this be Battle Stations this time?) and the crew had the missiles armed and ready in record time. Wally showed up, looked at the scope and the indicated hostiles heading towards us and went back to the field phone to tell the CP what was going on.

"Targets will be designated for Bravo One, Bravo Two and Echo Three." All three of us TCOs in the Rafha Cell acknowledged the message from the TD. It looked like there were going to be plenty of targets for everyone. The aircraft were headed right for our cell. Was it an attempt to get around the air defense network? Or were the enemy planes making a run for Rafha itself, figuring to knock out its airfield?

---

[37] Hawk missiles were steered by the wingerons (or "fins" to those who don't know the difference), which were in turn powered by on-board hydraulics. Since the missile is on a one-way trip the Raytheon engineers who designed it decided that a circulating system was unnecessary, so the missile ejects the fluid as it is used. If a plane maneuvers enough, the missile will run out of hydraulic fluid before it reaches the target.

[38] The penalty for celebrating with a bottle of champagne in the Kingdom of Saudi Arabia is death.

B-52S HIT IRAQI POSITIONS

116

At this moment a phone call came in. I had to turn the Conn over to Wally because I was needed for THAT STUPID GPS CLASS! I couldn't believe it! We were about to destroy an entire squadron of aircraft and I was needed to go to Bravo Two site to find out how to operate a GPS device.

But orders are orders. So I got into a vehicle with Specialist Gilbert and went to Bravo Two. I half expected to see the missiles begin taking off overhead, missiles I had been in control of just a few minutes before.

Once on Tapline Road we made our way East. I was looking at my map, still sulking at losing a chance to shoot something down when we started passing a French convoy going in the opposite direction. The drivers were unusually friendly, beeping their horns a little and waving in our direction.

Without even looking up from my map I said "I don't think they're waving at ME." Gilbert looked at me and then looked out the window and laughed. She even waved back at a few of them.

Once at Bravo Two I found out that there had been NO engagement, the aircraft turned back. Once again, we were cheated out of a chance to show the enemy and the world what we could do. The purpose of the phantom attack? As far as I can figure out it might have been an attempted retaliatory raid against a Saudi target which the Iraqis figured would have virtually no defenses. And normally they would have been right...

The GPS class was rather short because the practical portion of it was going nowhere. The Voyager device could not lock on to enough satellites to find our location.

"There's probably just too much interference in the area to get a fix," Tanis told us. "The manual is included. Practice with it and let me know if there are any problems."

Let him know if there are any problems? There was ALREADY a problem. Well, maybe I could figure out how to make it work if I had it long enough.

I got permission via radio to pick up mail at the battalion site, since another load had shown up since this morning. Just since our run in the morning there were more units setting up and the ones we saw previously looked like they had doubled in size. Tents were cropping up everywhere.

By the time we got the mail and got back it was dark, but I arrived in time for the BC's 1930 Key Personnel Meeting. This was one I'm glad I didn't miss: he outlined what the plan of attack was and what role we would soon be playing in it.

As soon as the ground invasion commenced (G-Day), which was currently projected to be about the middle of February, we were to break down both missile sites and move up with the 82nd Airborne Division and the 6th Light Division as they proceeded north along a road designated MSR Texas. This road would go to the small town and airfield of as-Salman, then proceeds to the Euphrates and Highway 8, a vital supply line between Baghdad and their forces in Occupied Kuwait.

"We will be moving up to positions on the Euphrates River," Captain Fletcher told us, "establishing defenses along its length."[39] Bravo Battery would be the spear point again, a job we were getting good at. "We will also have 'slices' from HHB and 34th Ordnance to support us until the rest of the Task Force can reach us."

Captain Fletcher turned to Ron. "It's possible that Bravo II might be airlifted to its next site via helicopter. 101st will be conducting an air assault all the way north. If the air assets are available then be prepared to take the bare minimum personnel you need to operate the system. The rest will come up in convoy with Bravo I."

On the CP's map an enemy unit was indicated. "The 45th Division is the only Iraqi formation between us and the Euphrates. It is made up of reservists and has been under constant air attack since the war began. It's not expected to put up much resistance."

Then the bad news: "Intelligence believes that chemical weapons have been distributed throughout the theater. There are several artillery units in this sector capable of firing chemical shells. It is not known whether permission has been given to the division commanders to use them.[40]

The meeting was very professional, very upbeat. We were all ready to cross into the Iraqi border and face the unknown.

I did try to make the Voyager work later. After reading the instructions ("Congratulations on your purchase of a Voyager Global Positioning System...") it was evident that this thing was simply not suitable for use under the conditions we had in Saudi Arabia. The book said not to operate it near large metal sources (like an Army truck), not to use it near running motors (like those found in an electric power generator) and not to get a fix near an electromagnetic source (such as one might find in a RADAR). The only thing I could figure was that this device was designed to be used by people in sailboats.

---

[39] These orders were later amended: we were to set up at as-Salman and provide an umbrella for MSR Texas and the Hawk and Patriot units moving into position on the Euphrates.

[40] As it turned out, Saddam DID give permission for his commanders to employ chemical weapons but by then communications between Saddam and his minions was in shreds. Besides, the typical Iraqi soldier was in far worse shape for dealing with a chemical environment than ours were.

THE AMERICANS
ARRIVE!

Needless to say, the machine could not get a fix while I was within the confines of the missile site, but it might do in a pinch to get the coordinates for a FUTURE missile site, so I continued to work with it. I walked out a hundred yards or so, but it still would lock on to more than one satellite, which meant it could not get a fix. I continued to walk until I could barely see the site.

I turned the Voyager back on waited. It picked up one satellite but nothing else. I placed the device on a rock and stepped away from it, figuring that perhaps my movements were "confusing" it. The Voyager still would not get that second satellite. Maybe the metal in my gear was interfering with it? I took off my protective mask carrier and LBE with its metal buckles and the holstered 9mm, placed them on the ground and 20 walked the device another feet away. Still nothing. I removed my belt with its metal buckle, my watch, my jacket, my hat and its metal rank pin, pens, pencils… I was leaving a trail in the desert but it simply wouldn't lock on to the locations.

I was seriously considering taking off my boots in case there was enough metal in them to throw it off when I finally realized the problem wasn't me, it was the device. I could stand naked in the desert and this thing wasn't going to tell me where I was. Another solution would have to be found.

Another night. I was watching my scope, with all the air activity to the north. There were Coalition bombers hitting tonight's targets, the occasional Iraqi fighter looking for an easy kill, unknowns…

And an Unknown which flew in my direction for a bit, then disappeared.

I looked at this for a moment and it reappeared, moved a little closed, then disappeared again. I blinked. Then I turned around and hit the siren. On the headset I told the crew to arm the missiles and get ready.

The TD rang up and wanted to know what was going on. "One-six, I have an aircraft attempting to fly under my coverage."

There was a pause. "Show me."

I use my azimuth cursor to locate the approximate point where the aircraft would reappear and sent a pointer. It obligingly showed up at the probable location, got closer, and disappeared again.

No doubt about it. That airplane knew I was here. He was making a beeline for Rafha I at a high rate of speed and at very low altitude. There was only one reason why an enemy plane would do that and that was because it planned to take us out.

"Weapons Control is 'Tight;' do not engage target." The TD pointed out needlessly.

"If it gets within self-defense range I will fire."

Saudi vegetable seller on the side of the road. Most of us had very little contact with the Saudis, if no other reason that there were so few of them.

Photo taken in Rafha, most likely. At the time I was fascinated by the whole atmosphere of the Middle East: the exotic garb, the strange language, the non-standard smells...

By now the BC was looking over my shoulders. The TD came back on. "Bravo One! Do not fire! That is a Friendly!"

"Bullshit! My friends don't fly under my radar at high speed." I was sweating as the range closed to self-defense.

"We have voice contact. Target is an F-16. He has battle damage and wants you to shoot down the MiG-29 behind him."

"The MiG-29 turned around several minutes ago! If you have voice with him, tell him to reduce speed and gain altitude."

Everything was ready. We were literally only seconds from firing when the unknown track began to change course and his speed started dropping.

From what I could piece together, an F-16 must have gotten separated from his wingman and was being pursued by a MiG-29. The F-16's IFF was damaged. The pilot was afraid that the Fulcrum would get him before he could return to friendly airspace so he came up with a plan: fly towards a Hawk unit and the Army would shoot down the pursuing plane.

The only problem was, no one let us in on the plan! We came very close to shooting down one of our own. In fact, we came closer to shooting him down the F-16 than we did the MiG-25.

In the meantime, Iraqi planes began fleeing to Iran. When Intel told us this we weren't sure what to make of it. The Iraqis had only reopened relations with their former enemy just a few weeks before. In doing so Saddam had granted many concessions to the Iranians, including waiving territorial claims, but had apparently gotten nothing in return. Could rebasing the Iraqi Air Force be part of some secret deal with the Ayatollahs?

Perhaps Saddam be planning a raid from Iranian territory, crossing the Arabian Gulf to hit Dhahran and other key targets in eastern Saudi Arabia? Or might the Iranians allow Saddam to operate from "safe havens" in Iranian territory, conducting hit-and-run raids against the Coalition and then fleeing across a border that the Coalition was not allowed to cross? This would have been very much like the situation in the Korean War, when MiGs operated from Chinese safe havens, protected from United Nations attack once they were over Chinese airspace.

Although no official word was sent down, it was generally accepted that there would be no political safe haven for the Iraqi Air Force. If those planes started attacking Coalition ground forces or attempted to shoot down our planes then they would be pursued and destroyed, regardless of where they were operating from.[41]

---

[41] The departure of IQAF aircraft to Iran might have been an attempt by Saddam to save some of his newer aircraft from destruction but he had not brokered a deal with the

Newspapers reported that Saddam Hussein, out of the goodness of his heart, authorized his pilots to suicide raids on Coalition targets. If the story was true then it was evident that most of his pilots were showing a distinct lack of initiative in this department.

Iranians before-hand. As a result, the Iranians kept the aircraft, declared them to be "war reparations," and repainted them with Iranian Air Force markings.

THE IQAF'S NEW MOTTO:

FLEE!

9. NEVER LOCK ON TO AN AWACS

The following day we had a NEW problem. The HIPIR was overheating. There had been an overheat indication overnight and the mechanics had put more glycol in the machine, but now the overheat problem was back. And now other fail indications were popping up.

It turned out that the source of the fail indications stemmed from the Army practice of putting glycol and battery acid in identical containers. When the mechanics were called to fix it in the middle of the night they picked up the wrong container in the dark. The acid not only failed to cool the system as well as the glycol did but also caused some sort of secondary damage. The technicians flushed the coolant system but some electrical problems were plaguing us now. Every day the enlisted radar mechanics, the warrant officers and even some civilian technicians came over and tried to nail down what was wrong.

In the meantime, my luck continued to hold. I was sent back to KKMC to pick up pay for the units. I went to battalion and hitched a ride with the pay officers from each of the other batteries. We drove over in a Suburban, a "non-tactical vehicle," so the long ride was comfortable. We picked up pay at a former bank in the Emerald City, the military complex in the center of KKMC, then stopped at the Air Defense Compound. I tried to get a few more maps from S-2, then went over to look up my old platoon leader from when I was enlisted. Captain Regan was working in the CRC, where the operational "map" of each missile system was displayed on huge plexiglass panels.

Patriot coverage was shown in blue fans, U.S. Hawks as green circles and Saudi Hawks in a third color and Marine Hawks in another. The Iraqi and Kuwaiti borders were "guarded" by a continuous line of circles and fans, including one that stood out: an orange circle, a bit bigger than the Hawk circles.

"The Syrians brought an SA-6 regiment with them when they sent an armored division." Captain Regan pointed to the circle. "Needless to say, it does not use the same IFF system as our aircraft and they're not integrated into the Net. We've been directing air traffic AROUND them."

So the Syrian Circle of Death is a de facto missile engagement zone, I thought to myself. Interesting. The SA-6 Gainful is a Soviet system which most closely matched Hawk in performance. "Do you think I might get a chance to get a tour of their system?"

"No. They're kind of touchy about the SA-6."

125

"Why? It's been around for years."

"Yes, but to Syria it's a secret weapon."

It was an interesting tour. The CRC was also tracking ground missions being sent into Iraq to locate and destroy the Scuds, since airpower alone was unable to get it done. "Scud-hunting" became a major pastime for our Special Forces troops and those of other Coalition members (such as the SAS). We saw many other nationalities at the base, including Poles, Brits, and Czechs.

While at KKMC we took advantage of our visit to go to the Big PX. Finding something you really needed might be a matter of timing... shelves were cleared off almost as soon as they were filled if it was a high-demand item. Things like radios, blankets, batteries, maps and film had to be purchased at the first opportunity... if you went to another aisle to get some Oreos those AA batteries might not be there when you got back.

Of course, there were no books. And not much in the way of drawing material either.

The road trip back to Rafha didn't get me back to our area until well after dark. The driver was unfamiliar with the area so I was doing my best to figure out how to get to the site. Part of the problem was that the few lights which would have normally been on, the TOC and antenna lights, seemed to be out. We finally made out the outline of tents and radar antennas and slowly approached. A pickup came towards us and I figured they were coming out to guide us into the site.

The pickup stopped abruptly and the doors flew open. Yelle and Harmon jumped out and, using the doors as shields, leveled their rifles at us.

I lowered a window and yelled out "Hey, it's all right! It's me, Lieutenant Crabtree! We just got back!"

For a moment I wondered if we were being robbed for the payroll. I don't know how far anyone would have gotten on the relatively small amount I picked up, though.

The two NCOs lowered their weapons. "You've got to me more careful, Sir." Sergeant First Class Yelle told me. "A lot of stuff's been going on."

The "stuff" Yelle was referring to was the Battle of Khafji. Iraqis had attempted to breach the Kuwait-Saudi border in at least three different places. Including one spot north of the intersection we had passed through just a few hours before at Hafar al-Batin. Two of the attacks had been blunted but the third, along the coast, had limited success in seizing the Saudi town of Khafji.

They wouldn't enjoy it long. A Marine team still hiding in the deserted town was directing airstrikes. The Gulf states would knock Saddam out of Khafji and back across the Kuwaiti border within a day or so.

One of the Stinger teams on alert near Radar Hill during Desert Shield. The team always had to be on the lookout for aircraft trying to fly under the Hawk's radar coverage.

A maintenance pickup parked at a launcher. This might have been one of the Alpha launchers, since the missiles were, at first glance, the same as the "standard" missile.

However, this had a predictable effect of putting units up and down the border on edge, ours included. Reports were filtering in of "strange vehicles wandering around units assembly areas and weapons sites." No wonder we were intercepted, after wandering back and forth in the desert with our headlights on.

The Iraqis seemed less and less inclined to fly, and even less eager to fight. It was just as well, as we were still having issues with the HIPIR and were frequently unavailable for engagements. Some of our coverage could be handled by Echo and AFP II but it would be better to have all fire units up. The technicians continued to tinker with the HIPIR.

Scud launches continued, but they were primarily aimed at Israel or at the cities of Dhahran and Riyadh. We rarely went on alert for scud launches anymore.

In the meantime, our maintenance personnel were still working on the HIPIR. At one point they thought they had it fixed, but in order to check it we had to lock on to a target.

There was no lack of aircraft within range of a lock, but the TD would simply not work with the AWACS to find me one. I sat in front of the display for an hour and a half and finally got tired of waiting. "The Hell with it." I said pointing out a track at random to the RO. "THAT one."

He nodded and I locked on to the aircraft. The energy readout in front of the RO went high. "Good, strong lock" Young said. Then his brow furrowed in slight confusion. "It's BIG. Multiple engines. Slow mover."[42]

What flies at slow speed in enemy airspace, is big and has more than two engines? Before I could work that one out I heard the TD yell "Break lock! Break lock! Don't you see the tab?!"

I put the HIPIR back in "standby" but the TD was still mad. "Do you know who you locked on to? That was the AWACS!"

Oooops. Well, it wouldn't have happened if they had given me an F-16 or a Tornado to lock on to when I asked.

"WHO locked on to the AWACS?"

"Bravo One." I responded.

"No, I want a NAME."

"Uh, Lt. Crabtree." Then I thought, if I'm lucky and it's not SERGEANT Crabtree by tomorrow morning.

Locking on to the AWACS was no joke. Well, not a very good one, anyway. If the Iraqis managed to get the Kuwaiti Hawks operational they could

---

[42] The HIPIR's radar beam acted as a carrier wave. The RO could actually hear the engines of an aircraft if he had a lock on it. A really talented could identify specific types of aircraft from their engine news, another valuable feature of the Hawk system.

try taking out our vital command and control system with it. And the AWACS wasn't in much of a position to figure out who was who up there.

One of our female soldiers was sent back because she tested as pregnant. There was a touching farewell as the other three females of the platoon saw her off, hugging her and crying.

The incident was not so sentimental with some of the other soldiers, who grumbled that if you were a male you here for the duration but if you were a female you had a "built-in" rotation policy. That was an unfair perception as virtually all of our female soldiers were better than that. But the fact remained that if a female got utterly tired and fed up with the routine of the desert they could go home with virtually no repercussions, despite general orders. And of course, there would not be a shortage of male "volunteers" to help her...

Everyone knew there was no punishment for getting pregnant. It would be bad for the Army's image.

During peacetime Hawk units simply do not have enough personnel to both operate the weapon system AND provide adequate security for the site. ADA missile systems occupy a lot of space but don't require a huge number of people to emplace and operate. So we were promised that in wartime we would get infantry support.

On February 11th we finally got our support: a platoon of soldiers from "A" Company, 1st Battalion, 22nd Infantry. The Army had pulled them from 10th Mountain Division and the men wore their distinctive crossed-ski patch and "Mountain" tab.

"Well, they won't be doing any skiing around HERE." Captain Fletcher said as they got off the truck.

The infantrymen were appreciated, even if some of them made it clear they didn't want to be stuck with us "Duck Hunters."[43] They aggressively patrolled the perimeter and improved our defenses. We in turn integrated them into our battery, training some of them to use the Stingers and also utilizing their lieutenant as a "spare" TCO on AFP II.

French soldiers began showing up at our site, interested in trading items. Some of the trade involved food, as the French rations were canned and

---

[43] I once got into a discussion about branch nicknames while on a truck during an enlisted leadership course. Actually, a field artillery soldier called me a duck hunter and I in turn called him a gun bunny, and the one Military Police soldier in the truck asked us why we were calling each other these names and we explained it to him. He then asked if there was a nickname for MPs. I looked at gun bunny and he looked at me and I finally said "Yeah, but we normally don't call you that to your face."

PSYOPS

included meat, fish and powdered soup. Some of them got Army PT shirts, hats and pins.

One tried to get me to trade my 9mm pistol. I didn't know how things worked in the *armée de terre* but I knew that if I didn't have that M9 with me when we got back home I would be on my way to Fort Leavenworth, and not as part of the staff.

But the French came up with an even more outrageous deal. While I was sitting in the CP the First Sergeant came in to talk to the BC. "Sir, you're not going to believe this."

"What is it?"

"Well, it's like this... the French want to trade a truck for one our females."

"They WHAT?!"

The First Sergeant didn't miss a beat. "Now, before you say 'no' remember we are short of towing pintels."

"They want to trade a HUMAN BEING for a truck?!"

"Oh, they don't want to KEEP her." The First Sergeant said. "They only want to BORROW her for a few days."

Captain Fletcher just shook his head "no" and that was the last we heard of the deal.

Damage to the HIPIR proved to be more extensive than initially believed. Apparently the battery acid had eaten seals within the coolant system and the radar could not be repaired without completely taking it apart. The secondary damage was from coolant leaking into the Electrical cabinets.

The HIPIR could not be repaired with the resources we had in-country. We were lucky, though... there was ONE spare in the entire theater, a "float" at KKMC. So once again I hit the road, this time in a five-ton truck. Staff Sergeant Carey and Sergeant Young went with me.

It was pretty uneventful until we reached the intersection at Hafar al-Batin. Nearby streaks rose up into the night in the distance as the sun set.

"MLRS?" Sergeant Young asked.

"They must be shooting someone up." I replied. The target was probably Iraqi positions in Kuwait.

We got to the site about 1900 hours. For some reason I had a feeling of dread in me that I couldn't account for but we pressed on.

There was some confusion when we arrived and I told one of the soldiers we were taking the HIPIR. "Oh, I think somebody picked that up and loaded it in a truck about an hour ago."

"Someone PICKED UP a multi-ton towed radar? And put it in the back of a truck?!" I asked.

"Oh," he responded calmly. "You guys must want the HAWK compound."

Sure enough, at yet another compound we found the float HIPIR. It was beautiful. It wasn't a rebuilt Phase II (which is what we thought we were going to get) but a brand-new purpose-built Phase III model. The mechanics started going over the radar doing acceptance checks.

The warrant officer overseeing the process had a hand-held radio and a scud warning came over it. An Iraqi weather radar had been detected. That was a bit odd, because the Iraqis had stopped giving away their intentions by radiating after the first few launches. The Iraqis might be a lot of things, but they weren't stupid. "We don't even worry about that unless they launch."

And that unexplained feeling of dread intensified.

The checks were all completed about 2100 and I was asked what I wanted to do: leave for the site immediately or stay at KKMC and wait until tomorrow.

"I want to head back right away." I answered. I wanted to get the new radar back to the Rafha I site so we could be operational as soon as possible but that feeling of dread influenced me as well.

I wasn't very popular for that decision and it WAS 0300 before we arrived back at the site but by noon the new radar was integrated and working. I was on shift when a casual announcement was made of the headset that there was another scud launch.

I asked the RO: "Who will it be today, Tel Aviv or Riyadh?"

It was neither. This time it was KKMC, and all three Patriot units in our sector were ordered to go to "Operate." Actually, the target area turned out to be Hafar al-Batin, which we had driven through. Five scuds were fired but none hit anything. Chalk one up for premonition.

As we prepared to cross the border the weather improved slightly. Temperatures had been dropping steadily (so much for that 120 degree weather we had heard so much about) and the light drizzle we had been seeing started to dissipate. We were wearing our new "cross-hair" parkas all the time now. I was lucky enough to have a DCU-pattern sweater I bought from a vendor. It was non-regulation but didn't look it so I could get away with wearing it.

CHEMICAL
WARFARE

Iraqi aircraft were still running for Iran or loitering at a safe distance away from the MIGCAP[44] and escort fighters. The thing was, the Iraqi aircraft would have had great difficulty even getting to our planes, since Soviet-style air defense fighters relied heavily on ground control interception (GCI) a system in which ground operators steered the planes to their targets. Like everything else the communists did, it was very centralized and relied as little as possible on individual initiative. But Iraq's GCI system had lost its radar vision and had great difficulty communicating with their aircraft.

Scuds were still being fired, despite our best efforts to find them and the Patriot interceptions which seemed to make them pointless. Units in quiet sectors (like ours) were giving up their PAC-2 missiles and sending them to where the action was: Dhahran and Riyadh. That left us with only a handful of PAC-2s and the rest PAC-1s but PAC-1s could be used in a pinch. Just not as effectively.[45]

And then there were other Iraqi weapons to worry about...

"NOW HEAR THIS!" I turned towards the sound of Lacher's voice as I sat on the steps of the PCP. "ECHO BATTERY HAS BEEN HIT BY A NERVE AGENT. THIS IS NOT A DRILL!"

I could see Echo's launchers and antennas from where I was sitting. Then I automatically closed my eyes, stopped my breathing, slipped my protective mask on, checked the seal. I was breathing through the filter in just a few seconds and I felt safe from the vapors. I ran inside the van and slammed the door shut.

Private Williams was the only one on duty in the van... at the time we were non-op because our IFF wasn't working. He was NOT masked and acted surprised to see me. "Are we masked? I heard on the headset that Echo got hit by something..."

"Goddamit, get your mask on!" I struck the switch which was supposed to activate the overpressure system, but nothing happened. The ONE time I really needed it to work...

And Williams was still maddingly screwing around with the headset. "Echo-One? Are you still on?"

---

[44] A Combat Air Patrol primarily concerned with MiGs, but would have gladly shot down Mirages or Sukhois if they made an appearance.

[45] PAC stands for Patriot Advanced Capability. Really, there was no such thing as a PAC-1 missile... a PAC-1 refers to the standard missile. The standard missile could be used to shoot down a scud thanks to a software upgrade. The PAC-2 missile was a refined Patriot missile with an improved proximity fuze and warhead.

"WILLIAMS, GET YOUR MASK ON <u>NOW</u>!!!" I found the circuit breaker which had tripped. I reset it and hit the overpressure switch again. With a soft roar filtered air began flushing the old air out.

Williams reluctantly put on his mask while I began prepping the system for an engagement. IFF or no IFF, if we had been sprayed by an Iraqi plane I planned on taking it out. The funny thing was, I hadn't heard any aircraft before this all started. Or artillery.

I called the TD, who said "Why do you sound muffled?"

"I have my mask on." I responded.

Over the headset I heard the TD say "Bravo-One, Zero-Six. Why are you at MOPP-4?"

"Report from Echo Battery indicates possible gas attack." I answered.

"It is highly unlikely that your area would be singled out for a chemical attack."

Well, I thought to myself, better to be cautious and alive than carefree and dead. "Maybe, but SOMETHING is going on. Echo is off the air."

Echo came back on the air shortly afterwards. "It's all right: one of the NBC alarms went off by accident and it scared one of the dogs. It started acting crazy, like it was exposed to nerve agent."

I was about to relay this info to Lacher when the field phone rang. Williams answered it and said "All clear. He says it was all a mistake."

"No kidding?" I said, pulling off my mask.

Everything was ready to go. All the minor problems with the weapon system had been resolved (except for the Alpha) and we all simply waited for the Ground War to begin. It was, if you'll pardon the expression, the "calm before the storm."

Our RSOP teams met at the intersection of Tapline Road and MSR Texas. My vehicle showed up first so while we waited I sat back and read my book…. Until the vehicle suddenly lurched as it was clipped from behind.

"It's OK, Sir." said Meister, who was driving that day. "It's just Lt. Riley."

Riley's CUCV pulled up alongside us. "Sorry about that," Phil said. "Didn't see you."

"DIDN'T SEE ME?!" I looked around. It was totally flat and there were absolutely no other vehicles in sight for miles in any direction along the straight roads.

I was still trying to figure that one out when a HUMMWV came into view and joined us. It was Captain Fletcher. "Have you seen Captain Pollard yet?"

"No, Sir. No sign of him."

IN THE FRENCH SECTOR

"Well, we're going ahead to recon the route."

Captain Fletcher moved on, checking the road and the designated holding areas on our side of the Iraqi border.

A French Land Rover pulled up next and one of their soldiers got out. "Hello!"

"Hello," I answered indifferently.

"Ticksis?" He asked.

"EXCUSE me?"

"Ticksis?" He gestured at the road. "Ticksis?"

"Oh. Oh, yes, TEXAS." I nodded my head and waved him north.

The French presence was rapidly making itself known. Columns of wheeled armored vehicles were lining up in places along Tapline Road flying the Tricolour. Nearby a French recoilless rifle team stood guard over the intersection. We even had a liaison officer assigned to us from the Foreign Legion, although the Legion has changed with the times and wear camo instead of those funky white hats.

One night something happened which illustrated how interconnectivity isn't always a GOOD thing. Sure, it allows me to "see" a potential target picked up 100 miles away, well beyond the range of my platoon's radars, but it also gave me a heck of a scare…

I was watching the display, with its Unknowns and Friendlies flying about. Hostiles were becoming rarer and rarer.

Which is why I bolted up a bit when I saw a diamond southeast of my location… BEHIND the defenses.

I got on the headset but other TCOs were already talking: "This is Charlie One, I see a Hostile…"

"Alpha One has a Hostile… how'd they get through the net?"

"Multiple hostiles! Is this an attack?"

"That's behind my Patriot site!"

The situation could have spiraled out of control fast but the TD stepped in and told everyone to stand by. There were dozens of Hostiles now but they didn't seem to be in a hurry, which seemed very odd. Eventually each one was replaced by a Friend symbol.

What caused this? What I was told later was that a Hawk fire unit had been airlifted into KKMC, had run through its operational checks and then integrated into the air defense net. After this staggering work the missile crew was ready to get some sleep but instead of manning the system or shutting it down they grabbed an Army private, had him put on the headset and told him

The author at the Rafha Site during one of the quieter moments. The author is wearing a highly-unauthorized sweater which was perfect for the conditions of the Saudi winter. No similar explaination can be found for the mustache. The IFF antenna has been removed from the van and is sitting on the ground.

to simply answer whenever the TD spoke to him. Then they left him to man the PCP by himself all night.

Well, after a while the private apparently noticed the TDECC's resemblance to a video arcade machine, only with a lot more buttons. He began moving the joystick around. He discovered that if he pushed down the stick when it was over a symbol he could make it flash. He later found out that if you pushed the button marked "Hostile" he could change all those circles and "U"s to diamonds.

And that's what he did, systematically changing the "True Friend" designation to "Hostile" on many tracks and at the same time sharing that information with the ICC, which shared it with other ICCs, which sent the information back down to fire units. I was told that when the problem was discovered someone was sent from the Air Defense Compound to physically yank the hapless private out of the van.

So because some soldier thought he was playing a really lame version of Missile Command or Space Invaders we believed, for few minutes, that our air defense net was compromised. Thank goodness the crew of that Hawk unit didn't hook up the missiles... we might have wound up with fireworks as well.

10. ONE BIG TRAFFIC JAM

23 February. It was G-Day -1. When I awoke I started collecting all my things. I "requisitioned" one of the "Hefty" bags[46] and rolled up both my sleeping bag and my foam mattress together in it, giving them some protection from the rain. I would have preferred to use one of the padded body bags but there were too few of them to go around.

We had some chicken, bought from a vendor in Rafha. While in the town I saw dozens of soldiers lined up to use pay phones. The pay phones were still working! I cringed when I thought of what was probably being said over them: "Hey Ma, guess where I'm going to be tomorrow... nope... nope... no, I'm going to be in a town called "Naziria" or something. No, that's not near Jersey City..."

The weather was turning back against us again. The light drizzle was just enough to make everything damp. We thought it might be an advantage to us as it might limit the effectiveness of chemical weapons. We took the little white pills which were supposed to help our system deal with nerve agent. We were given sealed MOPP suits to put on at midnight, replacing the ones we had been wearing on and off for weeks.

The following morning, G-Day, Captain Fletcher returned from battalion headquarters and briefed us on how the Ground war was going so far. The French had moved 30 kilometers inside Iraq, meeting little or no resistance. Our release time from our current mission would be about 1400.

We all clustered around radios. There was little news to report, but what there was of it was being repeated over and over again: Coalition ground forces were now inside Iraq and Kuwait, many prisoners were being taken, and there were few Coalition casualties. Also, there were no reports of chemical weapons being employed by Saddam. We kept our fingers crossed.

Things we didn't use every day were stowed away, as well as personal gear. The tents were brought down. We went ahead and took the camo off the vehicles.

---

[46] These were body bags sent to us in advance of the invasion. The nickname came from their resemblance to a popular brand of garbage bags.

IRAQI INTELLIGENCE

The only incident to put a little excitement into the process and that was when someone spotted the .50 caliber machine gun back in its ring mount on one of the trucks. We had gone ahead and removed it from the entrance to the missile site and this one soldier decided he would like to get a picture of him "manning" the fifty.

So his friend took his camera and stood out about 20 yards from the truck. The photographer was ready to get a great picture.

But what no one told the soldier in question was that the machine gun was not just mounted in the truck but loaded as well. When he grabbed the handles, which doubled as the triggers, he managed to fire a burst over the site.

Luckily, no one was hurt. Unluckily, the photo didn't turn out.

1400 passed with NO order to stand down and prepare to cross the border. NOW some of our soldiers were getting tense, wondering how long we would be delayed.

Finally, at 1600, the siren went off signaling breakdown. From the roof of B103 I could see the whole site and within minutes trucks were moving into the downrange area to get the missiles and launchers.

I hopped down, my forest green MOPP suit contrasting with the wet sand of the desert. The infantrymen were donning their masks and gloves. "Hey, it's all right," I told them. "That's just the signal for March Order. That's why everybody's running and the trucks are on their way down."

They unmasked, the squad leader muttering "It would be nice if you told us these things, Sir."

I'm sure the infantry squad spent the next several days cursing us air defenders. They were slated as replacements for the 101st Air Assault, should that unit take significant casualties, and some of them wanted to do some REAL fighting, not play bodyguard to our missile system.

The missile system was ready for movement in record time. Why not? After years of practice we were about to embark on a real, live shooting mission. Everyone lent a hand: systems mechanics helped with the radars, I helped the downrange crew get the missiles off the launchers, even the infantry guys helped with lifting and carrying.

I drove B103 to the entrance to the site, where the rest of the convoy would fall in on me. I had a small US flag flying from the CUCV's antenna; I figured if the French could fly their *Tricolour* there was no reason we should not fly the Stars and Stripes.

Bright orange-and-red signal tarps were placed on vehicle roofs and hoods to aid in our identification as "friendlies" so far as the Air Force was concerned. We were also given infrared-reflective strips for our individual

142

weapons and gear to help prevent us from being shot up by our own forces. We each put an IR square on top of our helmet covers.

The last of the vehicles rolled into convoy. Captain Fletcher took a few minutes to get everyone in formation and speak to us. He spoke to us of how proud he was of us and spoke with the confidence that comes from someone who knows his people and knows what they can do.

About 1930 we started to roll. We didn't have far to go: we pulled into a battalion assembly area. Our trucks were lined up and staggered. Captain Fletcher made some last-minute adjustments to the vehicles in the darkness and then we all went to a nearby tent for a hot meal: lunch buckets supplemented by granola bars, starburst candy and cartons of milk. Some of the candy undoubtedly ended up in the stomach of Scud, our mascot. That dog LOVED candy.

Originally we were supposed to move to the corps assembly area at midnight but this was pushed to 0800. We all crashed out as best we could, sleeping in the back of trucks or next to the vehicles.

After a little sleep everyone got up the next morning, G-Day +1. Heavier drizzle now. It almost rated the name "rain." Drivers started up their engines, doing checks. Some of the soldiers went to the tent to get some coffee. We were regretting the decision to take the cab covers off the trucks so we could employ air guards. It seemed highly unlikely that the IQAF would motivate itself to attack at this late date.

At 0730 Lt. Col. Kilgore came out to see us. The battalion commander had our mail with him and some new claymore mines. Wally decided to keep all the mines with him rather than distribute them.

FINALLY, we headed north again. We hadn't gone a kilometer before we reached the tail end of a medical convoy. From then on we would be stuck in a huge traffic jam as American units tried to catch up with the retreating Iraqis.

There was practically no traffic coming back south other than a few French vehicles (probably going back for resupply). On our side it seemed like every XVIII Airborne Corps vehicle was trying to squeeze into Iraq.

You could tell the road had been improved or rebuilt recently. Dirt mounds had been pushed on either side, where the road had been leveled. The surface felt solid and smoother than most of the hardball roads we had been on in Saudi Arabia.

We pulled over to eat at one point and we saw green buses heading south. As the first one passed we saw Arab soldiers in uniforms.

"What's happening?" Someone asked. "Are they sending the Saudis to the rear?"

Lt. Col. Walter F. Kilgore, battalion commander of 2-1 ADA. I was told later that he made a special effort to come out and speak to us prior to our movement into Iraq because heavy casualties were anticipated for Bravo Battery.

"Those are Iraqis!" I yelled, when I saw some of them wearing black berets.

The soldiers of Bravo Battery got their first look at the enemy. They were wearing olive-drab uniforms, a few looked haggard but most seemed happy. A few were waving at us as they headed toward Enemy Prisoner of War camps in the rear.[47]

One of the soldiers muttered "They'll have it better than WE will tonight."

"We're flying an American flag and invading their country and they're happy to see us?" I asked in disbelief.

"They're going south to safety and we're going north with missiles," TJ said. "Of course they're happy!" And he was right, after several weeks of bombing, artillery and strafing the Iraqis were no doubt ready for a break.

The EPWs were the cause of our traffic jams. In surrendering in such huge numbers they were tying down troops who had to process, collect, feed and transport them. They were accomplishing with a white flag what they could not do with their weapons: delay the Coalition advance.

Of course, that wasn't the only problem. We finally crawled far enough north to where we reached a checkpoint manned by MPs. I stopped and she asked for a form.

"WHAT?" I asked.

"Yes, Sir." She explained. "You have to have the same form as everyone else to get past this point."

"Soldier, are you telling me that the Army even has a form for invading another country?!"

"Sir, it's a DD1265, Request for Convoy Clearance."

I had to admit that I did not possess the all-important form. "But my battery commander or Captain Pollard might. We'll send somebody back to check."

Eventually, the vital DD1265 was found, annotated, stamped, logged and whatever else was necessary and we were allowed to proceed. When we reached the holding area we had only traveled 12 miles in 12 hours.

It was two more hours and then we were given access to more fuel. We rolled into an open area where the convoy parked. By the time the entire convoy was in place it was 0100 on February 26th, G-Day +2.

One of the green EPW buses took us to a tent area where they served us a hot meal. "Just think," I told Lacher. "You can tell everyone you were treated as well as a POW."

---

[47] Where each one was undoubtedly issued a DA2662 EPW Identity Card.

CONVOY

"If I was a POW," Lacher replied icily, "I'd be dry right now."

We drew hot lunch buckets, soup, pudding and M&Ms from a mess section which must have already served ten or twenty thousand meals since the Ground War began. I got some extra food for Tijerina, who was still with the RSOP vehicle, and the tired cook asked what kind of unit we were.

"We're Air Defense Artillery. Hawk."

"Well, go get 'em." She told us as we left.

Back at the vehicles Captain Fletcher had a plan. This was about the third he'd had since the convoy started but we listened. The Main Body of the convoy would not move up until 0900. However, B103 and a 2 ½-ton truck (B114) had permission to move up with another serial at 0530. I would locate the next missile site and the infantrymen in the truck would secure it. Captain Pollard was supposed to hitch a ride with us.

I climbed on the roof of the Blazer and tried to get a few hours' sleep. I must have been exhausted because I didn't wake up until Tijerina started the engine. I got out of my sleeping bag-mattress-body bag combo and tried to roll it it up in the dark but gave up and just tossed it inside the machine.

Wally guided us to the convoy we would be joining: a line of trucks carrying 8-inch gun shells.

Great, I thought to myself, I'm going to be staring at ten tons of high explosives the entire way north.

The road so far had been straight but now it got a little windy. Some of the bigger trucks had trouble negotiating the curves and one, a cargo carrier, was ditched on the side of the road. One of the ammo trucks had to pull over.

We were beginning to wonder how we would know when we were in Iraq. We knew we had to be close. We passed some sort of a concrete marker near an abandoned strongpoint. Piled rocks formed protected fighting positions. An abandoned volleyball net moved limply in the wind, which was growing in strength.

The road turned sharply east and we passed a second, much larger pylon. This one had a metal Saudi seal on it but nothing else indicated a border. I don't know what I expected: a fence, a wall, a series of stone markers?

We linked into a hardtop road. We had to skirt around a bomb crater at the very end of the road, no doubt a subtle suggestion from the Air Force telling the Iraqis "do not go past this point."

This meant we were now in Iraq.

Only a hundred yards further was an old guard post. A 1st lieutenant, an MP and a full-bird colonel were standing there and flagged us down. "Great," I told TJ, "they're probably going to ask for that damn form again."

"Were there any problems with the road?" the colonel asked when we stopped.

"Well, Sir," I replied, "we passed a ten-ton with a trailer ditched on the side of the road and an ammo carrier..."

"But there's nothing wrong with the ROAD, right?"

"No Sir. The road itself is just fine."

The colonel beamed. "Then go ahead and good luck!"

My guess is that he was either in charge of the engineer unit that had rebuilt the road or else was responsible for the route staying open. In either case, he did have a lot to be proud of.

Now we ran into the Mother Of All Sandstorms. Visibility was less than 500 meters and sometimes even less than 100 meters.

Despite the weather, the French continued to fly. Their helicopter gunships and transports sported white and black "invasion stripes" on their tail booms as they patrolled up and down the traffic jam, looking out for any Iraqi attempts to attack us. The pilots were either crazy or courageous or a little of both. Even when the sandstorm was at its peak they remained in the air, buffeting the helos and causing their tail booms to swing wildly to the left and right.

There was always the chance that there were Iraqi holdouts somewhere in the open desert. If they were out there the sight of hundreds of immobile vehicles would have been hard for them to resist. Of course, it wasn't as if we didn't have any teeth ourselves: if attacked we would have hit back with everything from M16s to anti-tank rockets.

The road was once again straight. We moved a kilometer or two at a time. We tried to pass the time by listening to the radio, but there were no English-language stations coming in on the AM or FM bands.

Visibility slowly improved in the afternoon as the wind died down. Captain Fletcher pulled up next to us. He said the rest of the battery was stalled as well, but several kilometers back. We got out the Slugger GPS to confirm our location (someone finally realized that the Voyager wasn't going to work) and discovered we still had 32 kilometers to go to our new site.

Suddenly, an entire aerial "column" of French helicopters passed us headed north: Pumas, Gazelles, even some Bo-105s. It looked as if they had a fire mission.

The soldiers in B114 finally managed to get the BBC on their shortwave: Saddam announced that he had "ordered his troops out of Kuwait." This was met with derision and laughter. Saddam announcing that he had ordered his

148

THE DAY YOU FIND OUT YOU'RE NOT INDISPENSIBLE.

troops out of Kuwait was akin to Hitler announcing he was unilaterally withdrawing from the Ukraine.[48]

A TV crew drove by at high speed on the left side of the road, endangering anyone who might have walked between the bumpers without seeing them, not to mention the danger from head-on collision. It looked as though they were filming the stalled convoy.

The infantry NCO in B114 was impatient to move up, as were all of us. He asked why we weren't moving. "What's the problem, Sir?"

I was standing a little off the road listening to the distant sounds of artillery. "Sounds like someone up ahead isn't convinced that the war is over yet."

"Well, why don't we just move off the right side of the road?"

I shrugged. "We'll just wait here."

"But we could go around!"

Now I was getting frustrated myself. "For all we know the sides of the road could be mined. Now, I'm not allowed to lose any vehicles, so unless you want to dismount your soldiers and have them walk ahead of my bumper…."

The sergeant didn't get out of the back of the truck. I went back to listening to the rumbling ahead.

At about 1700 the traffic jam seemed to finally break. The wind had died down too but it was getting cloudy overhead. We hoped to reach the new site before dark.

Now we began to see evidence that there had been an enemy here. We passed unmanned automatic weapons on sand berms, bunkers with empty gun ports facing the desert, unoccupied trenches heading away from the road. Anti-aircraft guns could be seen on nearby hills and forts formed by bull-dozers could be seen in the low ground. Tanks were parked in hull-down positions nearby. The barrel of every weapon was facing the same direction: south.

Few of the positions looked as though they had been fought over, although one did look like it had been singled out for punishment for some reason. Concertina wire formed temporary corrals for EPWs.

We began to see hilltops. This meant we were getting closer to our site. Lightning was flashing in the distance (or was it artillery?) when we reached the highest ground in the area. We dismounted at what would become Site 289.[49]

The area was pitch dark and rocks were evenly distributed throughout. It seemed like there was a ten-pound rock for every two square feet, which made walking very difficult. Stakes with chemlites were used to designate each

---

[48] Except for a few peaceniks in the States and Europe, I don't think anyone believed Saddam's spin on what was going on in Kuwait.

[49] Named for the altitude in meters. Bravo II was at Site 299.

spot where Hawk equipment was to set up. It was after midnight before the convoy showed up.

The convoy was no longer in proper road march order. Also, the vehicles sent to us by battalion added to the confusion, especially when some of their equipment turned out to have special technical requirements of their own.

Alignment was difficult in the dark and it seemed to take forever. It didn't help that we had gotten very little sleep since G-Day. By 0500 the site was fully operational and we were providing radar coverage from within Iraq. Exhausted soldiers were crashed out everywhere. I moved rocks so I could roll out my sleeping bag near the PCP.

The BC woke me at 0700 and told me he needed me at the CP. I stumbled over there after I grabbed my gear.

"We're expecting a movement warning order." He said. "The RSOP team needs to be ready to go in 30 minutes."

Another jump already! I figured things must be going incredibly well for us. We had already knocked the Iraqis back and now we were pushing hard to keep them off-balance. Then again, I didn't feel that steady myself but adrenalin took over as we collected up all the RSOP signs, fueled up the vehicles, and gave all the RSOP soldiers a "heads-up" of our next move.

When our 30 minutes were up Captain Fletcher got back with me: He had received the Movement Warning Order via secure radio (our communications were pretty sketchy the whole time we were in Iraq) and it looked like we would not be going out for a couple of days. But when we did go it would be to jump all the way to the Euphrates.

So I did a shift in the van and later drove with TJ and Specialist Brandenburg to scout out the as-Salman area. We drove to the south and saw the village of as-Salman in the distance. The 6th Light Division was already set up there and in various cantonments in the area. Then we headed north of the site. There was an area I called the Valley of Death where a battalion's worth of equipment was destroyed: armored personnel carriers, trucks, Russian jeeps and a few tanks. They must have been destroyed from the air. In one nearby area one of the "bunkers" turned out to be a disguised generator, complete with painted dark rectangles which looked like gun ports. It was the old generator-disguised-as-a-bunker trick.

Further up the road we spotted some tanks partially dug in. I told Tijerina to pull off the road and head in that direction.

"I don't want to run into any mines." He said.

"If there were any mines then there would be warning signs." I told him. Then I thought for a second: "But just in case, try to follow the tank tracks."

TJ just gave me a dirty look. He pulled up within 50 feet of one of the machines. "This is as close as I'm getting."

I climbed out of the CUCV. "Are you getting out?" I asked Brandenburg.

"Yeah. Sure. Why not?" he grabbed his rifle. "But if I had known we were going on an adventure I probably wouldn't have come."

The tank was an old Soviet-made T-55 painted a mottled green. I didn't notice any markings on the hull. As we cautiously approached I could see no obvious damage to the war machine. Ammunition still lay in crates next to the tracks and shells were lined up as if waiting to be loaded.

I thought every Iraqi tank for 100 miles around was destroyed but it suddenly dawned on me that we might have found an intact one. I pulled my 9mm pistol from its holster and told Brandenburg "Chamber a round. No point in taking chances."

We got to within a couple feet of the tank when it occurred to me that if someone was still inside this tank and they didn't want to surrender, a pistol and a rifle wasn't going to change his mind.

The tank seemed to be totally intact but empty. Another had a small hole punched in it and the interior was smashed up. The tanks formed a defensive circle of six. There was no sign of the "previous owners," our new nickname for the Iraqis.

11. LAUNCH!

February 28th, 1991. I awoke to the Queen song "We Are the Champions" playing on our PA system. "NOW what?" I asked out loud.

I collected my gear and walked over to the CP. Lacher told me the news: "A cease-fire is in effect. It's all over!"

We received new orders via teletype. Until further notice we would maintain our air defense coverage and be prepared to defend the sites from Iraqi stragglers who may have been bypassed and were unaware of the cease-fire. We would continue to provide Hawk coverage over the forward XVIII Airborne Corps elements until such time as those elements began withdrawing. Once we were given the word to withdraw we would return to our pre-G-Day positions.

We all congratulated ourselves for surviving the campaign with no casualties. We were truly amazed that chemicals had not been used against the Coalition. One might even be inclined to think of it as a miracle.

But a cease-fire did not necessarily mean the war was over. Iraqi aircraft were unaccounted for, so our Hawk battery remained in readiness. By-passed Iraqi troops were being found by other Coalition units all the time. We could not drop our guard.

Our soldiers were tired from the drive north and the missile equipment seemed a bit war-weary by this time too. The generators failed twice and it took almost a full shift for me to complete firing functions.

Now that the fighting was over we sent more patrols out to see what was in our new sector. Units were destroying any war material in the area as the former owners wouldn't be needing it any more. While some might call it "looting" we called it "bunkering," and it was a great outlet for the troops.

We scavenged a German-made mess trailer, complete with pressure cooker. This made a nifty trailer for hauling concertina wire. We found discarded gas masks made in Yugoslavia, complete with decontamination kits. Crated weapons were often marked as having come from Jordan.

Just before dark the Battery Commander returned towing a Chinese antiaircraft gun behind his HMMWV. It was a four-barreled antiaircraft machine gun, a Type 58. No one topped the BC when it came to bunkering. "We would have been back sooner but we had a Hell of a time figuring out how to lower its two wheels."

153

I took a look at the weapon. I never thought I'd ever see one of these things up close. And as I examined it I made a discovery…

"Hey, this thing is still loaded." I could see the rounds feeding into the chamber from the ammo boxes. "I could probably figure out how to clear it if you want…" I was somewhat of an expert on old-style antiaircraft guns, having read several books and examined many in museums. It was a hobby of mine.

Instead the gun was placed near the CP and the barrels aimed straight up. The BC didn't want anyone getting hurt. Especially me.

Later that night, during my shift, I went to the CP to find out how things were going. Collins was there and told me that he and Lt. Pace had found a tank earlier that day which was totally intact except for its missing swivel-mounted machinegun. Joe went inside the tank, trying to figure out how to remove the two coaxial machineguns. A French helicopter happened to be flying by when he popped his head out of the hatch.

The helicopter immediately changed course and began to make a run on the tank. It looked as though the French chopper was about to fire rockets at the machine. Joe did the smartest thing he could have done: he stayed right where he was. The helicopter slowed and then hovered for a minute, as if considering the situation. A window opened on the machine and someone took a picture of the "crazy American" and flew off.

There would be a lot of crazy stories like this one while we were in "Occupied Iraq." In another Lacher claimed that he and another soldier found a command bunker with maps and papers outside it. The soldier casually asked that "what's with all the balls?" The area they were in was covered with small, softball-sized spheres. They were bomblets dropped by the Air Force; in effect they were in a minefield and had to carefully back their way out of the area.

Yet another story some of our soldiers were inside a bunker and were collecting souvenirs when the military telephone rang. They looked at each other, then one picked up the handset and heard a voice speaking in Arabic. They yanked the wires and then tried to trace it. The wire went off into the open desert. Chief Dungy collected several Iraqi phones and used them to supplement our battery communications.

The further from the main road you went the more intact the Iraqi bunkers were. Some positions still had food stashed in their central bunker, usually canned Kraft cheese, rice and a few tomatoes. We were told not to eat the cheese, which had the Kraft logo in Arabic. There was a fear that the Iraqis, who apparently had their own Kraft canning plant, had introduced some sort of biological agent into the cheese and had deliberately left the cans behind,

DEBRIS

knowing we would find them and eat them. It was the old poisoned-cheese-in-a-can trick.

This sounded like an extremely unlikely plan. However, a few of us did end up eating the cheese and none of us showed any signs of being exposed to a biological agent… unless another part of the cunning plan was to have us immobilized by the discomfort of constipation.

We tried to use one of the Iraqi trucks. It ran, but just barely as it belched smoke. It had something to do with the poor quality of fuel the Iraqis used. We ended up driving the thing over a cliff (safely, of course).

Someone told me that an SA-6 site was located near the airfield of as-Salman. I thought to myself that this might be a great opportunity to see one of these Soviet surface-to-air missile systems up close but Lt. Pace told me not to bother. "There's nothing left to photograph."

A supply depot of some sort was found and Iraqi uniform items brought back to the site. Everyone at our site had an olive-drab Iraqi cap if they wanted it. Some of the jackets were made in Romania. The tags stated they were intended for the "Popular Army."

We also found personnel files. We had a record of many of the soldiers in the 45th Division, including unissued ID cards and Xerox copies of passport information. Someone suggested we should send these back to S-2.

"Why?" asked the BC. "If we need information on these guys we'll ask the soldier in person in an EPW camp somewhere in the rear."

Bunkering became much easier when we discovered that the Iraqis had buried their personal weapons in a certain location relative to their CP bunker. Every day our vehicles brought back AK-47 rifles, machine guns and even some RPGs, along with discarded helmets and load-bearing equipment. Laid out near the Motor Section, the area looked like a Kabul bazaar or a Kentucky knife and gun show, what with all the military collectibles and weapons we had lying about.

It seemed as if the further we got from our battalion headquarters the better equipped we were.

The next morning I asked permission to try to clear the Type 58 but the BC told me that he decided to let the Infantry tow it to the Crater, a large depression located behind the battery area. There they would figure out how to clear the four machine guns. "They deal with heavy weapons more than we do."

Suddenly there was a heavy crack of automatic fire. "What was that? The BC asked.

"Sir, that would be the Infantry clearing your gun." They might not have been familiar with the Type 58 but they enthusiastically got to know it better, firing several dozen more rounds from it. After the security section had their fun

156

FOOT TRIGGERS

the weapon was towed to the entrance to the site, where it served to augment the ground defenses.

This place was like Infantry Disneyland: all kinds of things to shoot. I think everyone who wanted to had the opportunity to fire the AK-47 at our impromptu "range." I can tell you it's a great close-in weapon but I would rather have an M16 if I wanted to reach out and touch someone. I also shot a small-bore machine gun recovered from a tank, hitting some ammo boxes despite an improvised mount and a lack of sights.

I didn't try to fire the RPG-7, though... my Russian wasn't up to translating the instructions. It was good enough for another item though.

The First Sergeant dropped off some more stuff at the site after a run. It included a pistol and some shotgun cartridges. I picked up the weapon and looked at the Soviet markings. My Russian WAS up to reading the Cyrillic markings on the device. "Oh, wow! A very pistol!"

"A what?" the First Sergeant asked.

I picked up one of the "shotgun shells," opened the breech of the pistol and slipped it in. I closed it and aimed it upwards. When I pulled the trigger a green streak flew upwards.

"It fires signal flares." I said needlessly. "Hey, do you think I could keep this?"

He shrugged. "Sure!" With all the AK-47s, machine guns and RPGs lying about, it was no skin off his nose if the crazy eltee wanted to keep a flare pistol for a souvenir.[50]

I fired off several more flares until a French helicopter flew over the site to see what the Hell was going on.

Kuwait was liberated and we were getting confirmation of the atrocities committed by the Iraqis during the last few months. Graveyards full of Saddam's victims were found. Torture, rape, pillage and murder seemed to be the norm for Saddam's short-lived "19th Province."

While the Kuwaitis were celebrating there were also tales of retribution. Apparently some Palestinian refugees who had been granted residence in Kuwait showed their gratitude by collaborating with the Iraqis, turning in people sought by the secret police and assisting the Iraqis in their large-scale looting. In

---

[50] We ran into another Catch-22. Initially, I was told that we couldn't bring anything back unless it was rendered inop. When we told them we had the means to do that with the tools and equipment we brought with u, we received instructions that we had to fill out a DA 7579 Demilitarization Certification and Verification Certificate and present it with the device. Needless to say, we did not have this particular form with us when we departed Fort Bliss.

return, the Palestinians were treated pretty much as Quislings when the Kuwaitis got their country back.

In our area, there were hardly any signs of actual resistance to the Coalition offensive by Iraqi ground forces. Most of the damage to the Iraqi positions appeared to be from aerial bombing, although some tanks and vehicles showed signs of being hit by tank fire. They may have been hit after being abandoned or in some cases appeared to be trying to withdraw. In our area we saw no bodies of Iraqi soldiers, although our own graves registration folks might have recovered them before our arrival.

On one of my bunkering runs I came across something very odd. We were in a headquarters complex of some kind, and we found various bunkers with papers but not much else of interest. I rested my hand against one of the sandbagged bunkers and thought to myself that it was odd that the sand would be so HARD.

I pulled out my knife and cut the fabric. It didn't contain sand, it was concrete. The Iraqis had poured concrete into sandbags and laid them the same way they did ALL their sandbagged bunkers. This made the bunker much more survivable without attracting any undue attention.

Which begged the question WHY?

I went around and found the entrance. I very carefully walked down the steps... and found a high-ceilinged room with a long wooden table and something like 20 chairs. Each chair was set the same distance away from the table's edge, about six inches. It was the officer's mess and it looked as if they planned on coming back. It gave me the creeps for some reason.

Nearby we found what must have been the CO's personal bunker, with a bed and a desk. He even had a personal shower, a real luxury in the desert. It was already looted so I didn't get any souvenir of interest there.

I learned later that few of the officers were captured when we moved into Iraq. It appears that many of them placed themselves on leave right when it started getting interesting, and tried to make it to the Euphrates. They left their soldiers to fend for themselves.

Pictures of Saddam were everywhere: pictures clipped from magazines, posters, even a semi-permanent monument. He posed as a sheikh, a businessman, a military commander, Big Brother (those were the ones where the eyes followed you), and statesman. There were no pictures of him holding a gun in one hand and a hostage in the other, which I personally felt was an oversight.

At an Iraqi antiaircraft artillery site I saw what happened to guns which shot at Coalition planes. Totally intact guns had their ammunition still sealed in weather-proof canisters. Individual guns which had their canisters opened, with

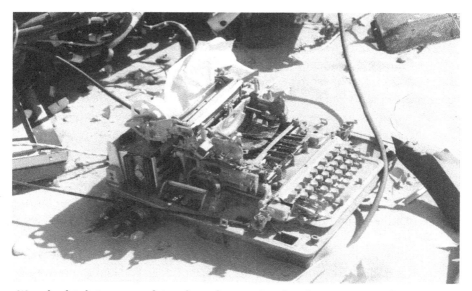

Wrecked teletype machine found at an Iraqi radar site near the border. The entire site was pretty much a debris field. Most of the equipment used at this site appeared to be Soviet.

Photo found in one of the bunkers of an Iraqi soldier posing with his AK-47. Thousands of these men were captured just in our sector. Many of them had Saddam mustaches of one kind or another.

the intent to use the ammo to shoot down planes, were hit at least once by bombs. The intact guns had the gun sights (which were removable) taken by other souvenir hunters; one of the flattened guns had its site thrown 50 feet away. This became my souvenir.[51]

I returned from another bunkering run and discovered that something was up. One of the 34th Ordnance soldiers told me that Bravo II had accidentally fired a missile.

"Yeah, right." I responded. I knew how many safeties were in place to prevent an accidental launch. I figured someone was pulling my leg. But when I got to the CP I discovered it was true. At about 1600 the missile had been fired during regular systems checks. We got the rest of the details after a while, and it became obvious that it was one of those things which could have happened to ANY of us TCOs, given the circumstances.

The firing was a result of a series of mistakes, any one of which should have been inconsequential, but together had circumvented the safeguards and had made it possible to fire an actual missile during firing functions. Mistake Number One was the fault of the downrange crew. They decided not to disarm the missiles, nor did they insert the safety keys. They ran firing functions on Launcher One, letting the fire commands go to simulators attached to the launcher's umbilical cables. Once Launcher One checked out, the crew hooked the umbilicals back to the Hawks, relying on the junction-box operator to disable the launcher according to Standard Operating Procedures (which they themselves were not following, by the way).

At the J-box the operator made Mistake Number Two. Misunderstanding his instructions, he enabled Launcher One AS WELL as Launcher Two, returning it to "operate" instead of leaving it in "safe." Launcher Two was now equipped with simulators, but Launcher One now had live missiles hooked into the system.

Mistake Three, the final mistake, was made by a lieutenant in the Platoon Control Post. He failed to note on his panel that he had two available launchers, not the one he should have had. Also, Launcher One indicated three missiles available where there should have been zero.

"Three, two, one, fire." He "fired" the simulator on Launcher Two. The downrange crew noted that the launcher responded correctly, providing super-elevation and lead angle. After a moment it lowered itself back into ready position.

---

[51] I still have this, mounted on a wooden base.

Meantime, the ADP, the electronic "brain" of the Hawk system, noted that although a fire command was sent to and received by Launcher Two a missile did not actually leave that launcher. In accordance to its programming it considered Launcher Two to have a failure which might affect its performance and "looked" for another launcher to switch to. I can only assume that this Cold War programming was designed to free the TCO from tracking status on every single missile on his board during active engagements with enemy aircraft which might manage to cause some damage to the system due to enemy gun or missile fire.

Normally during firing functions the ADP would not have an alternative launcher to switch to and would have remained on Launcher Two, the only available launcher. But because of the errors already made, Launcher One was available. The ADP automatically switched from Launcher Two (the "damaged" launcher) to Launcher One. The lieutenant did not notice. "Three, two, one, fire." He pressed the button. The command went through the J-box, directly to the launcher and on to a missile. To the horror of the downrange crew, Launcher One responded by super-elevating and providing lead on the imaginary target. Once the launcher was properly positioned the firing circuit was completed through the umbilical and the solid rocket motor ignited on the selected Hawk missile. One of the crewmembers was just a few feet from Launcher One when the missile streaked off the rail, quickly reaching Mach 2.5.

The accidental launch resulted in an incredulous pause, then a flurry of panicked activity at Site 299. The lieutenant left the van to see for himself what had happened. Soldiers ran out of vehicles and tents to get a look at the finger of smoke pointing upward in the sky. And the platoon leader, Lieutenant Ron Williams, rushed into the van to press the self-destruct button, hoping to avoid accidentally hitting one of our own aircraft or caused some other kind of mischief. Crewmen checked on the downrange personnel to see if they were hurt (they were not) and the Infantry guys just cheered. "Do that again!" one of them yelled.

The launch was detected by AWACS. This information was relayed to directly by radio to 11th ADA Brigade's TOC at KKMC. And then Brigade called down to 2-1 ADA battalion to ask "What the Hell is going on up there?!" This was relayed to us via a furious teletype message.

Over the next several days an investigation was initiated, DA 2823s[52] were filled and everybody in the chain of command came out to see for themselves what had happened. Captain Fletcher drove out to Site 299 the same day. The following day a helicopter brought up Lt. Col. Kilgore. The day

---

[52] Sworn statements.

RPG

after that it was Colonel Garrett, the brigade commander. The day after that it was some general from XVIII Airborne Corps.

"At this rate," I told some soldiers as we watched the latest batch of officers land, "General Schwarzkopf will be here the day after tomorrow."

The worst part of it was, the mistake the lieutenant made was an easy one to make; in peacetime, every TCO I had ever met had done it at least once. Hell, I had done it. The only difference was that when I did it we were training with simulators. The lieutenant had the misfortune of doing it while he had live missiles hooked up.

Had the accidental launch taken place anywhere else but southern Iraq, and any other time except the tenuous cease-fire, punishment would no doubt have been swift and wide-ranging. After all, the missile had cost the American taxpayers $250,000. Instead, the "Crew of Shame," as a few people called them, were allowed to redeem themselves.

Once we were back in the U.S., the launcher was painted with a stencil that read "Launch, 2MAR91, Iraq." It was always used in ceremonies requiring a Hawk launcher.

Later that same evening as the launch, Captain Fletcher ordered the battery into MOPP level One. S2 informed the BC that Iraqi prisoners had told of a plan to employ chemical weapons that night. It seemed that it was Iraqi self-preservation rather than American skill at interrogation that brought the plan to light: Upon surrendering, EPWs were asking for French or American protective masks to replace the shoddy ones they had been issued.

The story told to Coalition intelligence officers was that a chemical attack had been planned for March 2nd. It was unclear as to whether or not the attack might still be carried out since the Iraqi command and control network was in shambles. Many units were unaware of the cease-fire and others equipped with chemical weapons might not receive the order rescinding the attack.

Just after midnight there was a knock at the PCP door. It was the French liaison officer. He told us that their radar was picking up unknown helicopters. "Are you picking up anything to the northeast?"

"No, but a low-flying helicopter would have to be pretty close for us to see him." I answered. "How far out was he?"

"Forty kilometers."

I frowned. "In this terrain we might see him at thirty." I would have liked to just bring the French officer in, but security restrictions prevented it. While the French had Hawk they did NOT have Alpha and there might be some uncomfortable questions about what the extra gear in the van was for.

"Well, two gazelle helicopters have been sent. They have the valid codes," he said in a way that made it clear he was concerned for their safety.

"OK, thanks. We'll look out for them."

The French officer nodded and ran back to his vehicle and his radios. I closed the door and got back on the headset. "Three-Zero, Bravo-Two, this is Bravo-One. French report unknown helicopters to the northeast." I looked at my scope but there was nothing coming in on the CWAR.

Three-zero responded, "Roger, Zero-Eight. Datalink with AWACS is still down."

Damn, I thought. Of course.

I switched to intercom and told the J-box "The French say we've got some unknown helicopters out there. Look sharp and keep everybody clear of the downrange."

"Roger! Downrange area clear."

I couldn't help smiling. "We've been through all this before."

"That's for sure." Replied Sergeant Young, without taking his eyes off his scope.

There were no targets in the northeast, but there was a jam indication. Something was out there, trying to interfere with our radar.

More beating on the door. This time the French officer sounded a lot more concerned. "There are troop movements and helicopters converging in on our positions. The whole division is on alert!"

"I've got a jammer in that area," I replied. "It might be something but so far no definite targets. Let me know if you find out anything else."

I returned to the scope. NOW we were getting a target, one that would disappear, then reappear a few seconds later, just a little bit closer. The target appeared to be using terrain masking to come in under our radar, a maneuver a friendly aircraft would not do, especially with every Iraqi radar between us and Baghdad knocked out.

"It looks like they're homing in on the PAR." SGT Young reported. And he might well have been right: we had reason to believe that some Iraqi helicopters had been modified as a kind of low-speed Wild Weasel, carrying enough jamming to disrupt a specific system then firing an ARM in to destroy it.

It wasn't worth the risk. "I'm dropping the PAR." I reached up to the control panel and shut it off with a single push of a button. "It won't do us any good against helicopters anyway."

Lieutenant Fecteau was monitoring over the headset. "This may be a silly question, but can you get a TAS lock on these targets?" She was hoping that the Tracking Adjunct System camera attached to the HIPIR might give us a good look at them.

CHECKING THE AREA
FOR VERMIN

"That's a negative." I told her.

Sergeant Young agreed. "We've got the cheapest model available. No infrared capability."

"That wouldn't do us much good anyway." I added. "What's the silhouette of French helicopter going to tell us?" We still wouldn't know if it was one of OUR French helicopters or one of THEIR French helicopters.

Suddenly a target popped up within five kilometers of us, moving at high speed right towards our position. Self-defense criteria clearly stated that we would have to practically be bombed by a plane pulling a 40-foot flag in broad daylight piloted by Saddam Hussein himself before we could shoot at him, but I wasn't taking any chances. I hit the siren.

The target was still out there, popping in and out, when Captain Fletcher came in to see what was going on. I quickly briefed him on the situation.

The BC wasn't entirely awake, but he was conscious enough to give me an order: "Don't fire on him!" he told me, indicating the unknown.

"I'm not, sir, but I'm going to be ready for him in case he tries anything."

The situation slowly, very slowly, defused. The unknown helicopters disappeared back into the night. The Iraqi troops headed away from our lines. And the expected chemical attack never came.

General Schwarzkopf met with Iraqi military representatives at the Iraqi village of Safwan, between Kuwait City and Basra. The Coalition weaponry, M1 Abram tanks, M2 Bradley AFVs, Apache helicopters, Patriot missile launchers, that made Iraq's defeat possible was put on display for them to see: the only thing missing was a fly-by of Coalition airplanes, but that was cancelled as unnecessary; the Iraqis had already seen enough of our planes to last a lifetime.

BBC news was now hooked up directly over the headset. We listened to reports that the first of our POWs had been released. There was also a news item on the revolution in Iraq: it seemed that the Kurdish minority in the north were making a go at getting rid of Saddam and his henchmen once and for all. In the south, the Ba'athist dictatorship was losing control of the areas inhabited by the Shi'ite majority. At the time, Saddam's regime seemed to have just a few days or a couple of week's existence at the most.

I was pulled off shift by Lieutenant Whitmire to investigate a mine incident that took place in which an HHB vehicle had been damaged. The driver pulled off the road and felt something explode under the pick-up truck. It shredded the tires and bounced the front end of the vehicle, but otherwise hardly damaged it.

Someone in the chain of command wanted the location identified and marked. Suddenly, I was the one person in the battery who really knew how to operate a GPS. I should have felt special.

I found Sergeant First Class Tijerina in the GP medium. "Come on, we got a mission." I told him.

"Where are we going?" He asked as he started to get off his cot.

"We're going to go look for a minefield."

TJ started to lie back down on the cot. "Gee sir, I've been driving ever since we got here. Why don't you take Wailikainen?"

Specialist Wailikainen, sitting on another cot, was surprised to find himself nominated for the job. "Huh?"

Our route took us south of Site 289 along MSR Texas. Eventually we overshot the area where the mine incident took place and reached an Iraqi radar site. We drove in a little closer so we could get a good picture of it.

I later learned that this site was part of an early-warning network and the first target hit inside Iraq. Struck by fixed-wing and rotary-ring aircraft, the loss of the site produced a "hole" in Iraq's radar coverage, a hole through which much of the Coalition air armada traveled on its way to other Iraqi air defense sites. Its destruction led to the unraveling of Iraq's air defense net.

The area had taken massive hits. One of the concrete buildings at the radar site had a huge hole in the roof where a bomb had entered. Nearby radar vans had been chewed up by gunfire, probably by an A-10's Gatling gun. To make certain that the site could not be re-used, several cluster bombs had been dropped, as evidenced by the empty casing scattered about and clearly marked as anti-personnel cluster bombs. Destruction was total.

We turned back north and after a short while came upon the location of the "mine." Although we couldn't identify the exact spot where the explosion took place, the area where we were had no defensive positions for a minefield to support. In fact there did not seem to be any other mines at the location. The report I sent up stated that the vehicle was probably a victim of one of our own bomblets, originally intended for the radar site but dropped short or thrown clear of the target. This would explain the small size of the explosion and why there didn't seem to be any other explosive devices in the area. Nevertheless, the site location provided by the GPS was sent up the chain.

The day after a big sandstorm, while Lieutenant Pace and myself were in the CP, one of the infantrymen told us they had found a bomb nearby. "Where?" Joe asked.

"Near the showers."

"How could there be a bomb inside the site"? I asked. "It was cleared before we moved in."

"It was attached to a parachute; it must have blown in with the storm." The Infantry guy smiled. "Can we blow it up?"

"Mark it and make sure no one goes near the thing." Joe told him. He knew that if it was one of ours moving it could be extremely fatal.

"But we already moved it down into the crater."

"You WHAT?" I yelled as I turned to face him. "That's crazy! The thing could have been equipped with an anti-tampering device!"

I was really mad. The thought of someone getting himself killed after the war was over, especially with something dumb like playing with a bomb, just bugged the hell out of me.

We were lucky no one was hurt. An EOD guy came by later, looked at the information we collected on the bomb, and just shook his head. He didn't go down to the crater to get a closer look.

Every day brought explosions and plumes of smoke. The Coalition was about to leave southern Iraq, having accomplished the mission of liberating Kuwait. We were destroying whatever might be of military value within occupied Iraq. Then we would consolidate our equipment and prepare for our return back to the States.

12. AFTERMATH

My little ADVON group departed Saudi Arabia after a long trip back from Iraq. Our route took us to Rome, Ireland and, finally, Fort Bliss.

The reception was overwhelming. As we exited the Boeing 747 people were lined up on either side of the walkway leading to the hanger. I never in my wildest dreams thought that there could be such a welcome home. Signs, balloons, yellow ribbons, and banners were everywhere.

Maj. Gen. Donald Lionetti, the Chief of Air Defense Artillery, was there to address the returning troops, telling us how proud he was of the "heroes of Desert Storm." It was odd to hear ourselves referred to as heroes. I know that I personally did not feel like a hero (whatever THAT's like) but I did act professionally and did the job that needed to be done. However, the U.S. armed forces as a whole had accomplished something heroic. We had moved an army into the desert, supported by firepower from the U.S. Navy and the Air Force, and had defeated a huge enemy force. Our enthusiasm was high, because we were well-trained. Our strength was great, because of the lavish attention spent on the military during the Reagan Era. And our morale was excellent, because we had confidence in our own abilities and the abilities of our Coalition allies.

Later, there would even be a victory parade in downtown El Paso. Once again I was in the wrong place at the wrong time and missed out on marching in that one (I think I was on 24-hour duty or something). It didn't matter... I thought it was great that our soldiers were being recognized for the awesome job they had performed.

Meanwhile, back in Iraq, Saddam was allowed to keep his helicopters. He was also, in short order, given back his captured soldiers (the Saudis politely called the EPWs "guests") and after a few threats were given rifles and told to shoot their fellow Iraqis, who had risen up in opposition to his dictatorship. Saddam crushed the resistance bloodily and over the next ten years he would play a cat-and-mouse game as to whether he did or did not have various weapons of mass destruction.

But if you had asked me at the time I would have bet money that Saddam wouldn't last more than a couple of weeks. Like a lot of people, I underestimated just how ruthless and determined Saddam was. We might have won the war but no one ever seemed to get around to telling Saddam he had lost it.

Soldiers and their bags waiting at KKMC for their outbound flight. We were subject to customs inspections before we boarded and I saw one MP pull a machete out of a duffel bag.

On board the flight home. I never noticed at the time how many different emotions could be read on these faces.

For a while, Air Defense Artillery enjoyed an unprecedented amount of *esprit de corps*. At the time of Desert Storm ADA was a relatively new branch of the Army, having split from the Artillery branch in 1968. This was the first opportunity ADA had to demonstrate what we could do.[53] Now we had a credible combat record. Not only had Patriot units intercepted enemy ballistic missiles for the first time ANYWHERE, other ADA weapon systems had provided a shield for Coalition forces, preventing Iraqi air strikes and surveillance. What's more, the air defense assets had kept up with tip of the spear, a neat trick in itself given the speed of the Coalition advance.

It was a good time to be an Air Defender. The Fort Bliss Officer's Club commissioned an 11th ADA Brigade Desert Storm mural, part of which was based on a photo I took of our missile trucks arriving near the Iraqi border after the Big Jump. There was a special commemorate book published highlighting each battalion's participation in Desert Storm and Desert Shield. Our unit colors were given streamers for their participation in the war and 11th Air Defense Artillery Brigade was presented the Valorous Unit Award, the unit equivalent of a Bronze Star. We were all authorized to wear the 11th ADA Brigade's patch on our right arm, making it a "combat patch." There were "scudbuster" shirts, pins and patches, all of them featuring the ADA crossed cannons and missile insignia.

Patriot launchers which actively engaged enemy scuds were even decorated: they were discretely stenciled with dates in which they launched missiles at the enemy, in the same way we had noted the date of the accidental launch in Iraq. Not quite the same thing but something that should be remembered nevertheless.[54]

U.S. Route 54 was renamed the Patriot Freeway in honor of our role in Desert Storm. This road went right past Fort Bliss into the desert where so much of our training took place.

Air Defenders felt pride in their Desert Storm service. Some officers and NCOs kept and mounted twisted metal pieces of scud missiles recovered after attacks on their defended assets. If you were there they were relatively easy to get: debris often fell on airfields and other potential targets and had to be cleared with bulldozers from what I was told. A part of a missile fuselage on your desk made a great conversation piece.

Things seemed to be looking up for the future of our branch. With proven antimissile technology it was felt that the next step was to create a

---

[53] The last time an enemy aircraft was shot down by U.S. antiaircraft fire was during the Korean War.

[54] It was over ten years before there was any public discussion of the accidental launch. The Army was willing to volunteer that information at the time.

BAGHDAD

National Missile Defense which would not prevent an all-out nuclear attack (which some argued would be "destabilizing") but could prevent the United States from being blackmailed by a country possessing just one or two nuclear missiles.

However, the euphoria didn't last. Everyone in the media seemed to be committed to picking apart Patriot's performance during the Persian Gulf War, as it was then being called by some people. Some of the criticism was valid... the Patriot system often hit the target selected but sometimes the warhead would survive the interception and explode on impact. Critics pointed to this as a failure and tried to make it seem as if the entire weapon system was a waste of taxpayer funds. The same people who built up Patriot as a miracle weapon were now doing their best to convince everyone it was a piece of junk.

Even while the media criticized Patriot's recent performance a new Patriot round called a GEM[55] was in the works. It was based on lessons learned from scud intercepts and would be capable of destroying Saddam's missiles, should they be launched again.

No one in the Big Army seemed to be willing to stand up to the critics of Patriot's performance record... instead, they just wanted the topic to go away. This was the beginning of a downward slide for morale. It didn't help that Patriot units remained in the Middle East even as the rest of the U.S. Army's units were withdrawn. Why? Well, Saddam might still have some scuds hidden that our satellites and the arms inspectors haven't found.

"But I thought Patriot didn't work." Some private was bound to ask.

"Shut up and get on the plane," was the answer from Big Army. Every Patriot battalion would end up rotating into Saudi Arabia and Kuwait under Operation Southern Watch, an operation most Americans never heard of. Worse, the rotations didn't count towards overseas duty so you could do these rotations virtually back-to-back and still wind up doing a tour in South Korea.

Patriot units went from being Saddam's nemesis to being his yo-yo.

And the hits kept on coming. U.S. Army Patriot soldiers sent to Israel during Desert Storm were awarded the Anti-Aircraft Warrior Badge by the IDF. At that time many foreign awards were authorized by the Department of the Army for wear on both BDUs and dress uniform and there was a precedent for Air Defenders receiving such a badge, as a result of working with our German allies, but not this one. For whatever reason the IDF badge would not be permitted for wear by ADA units who had earned it. This was yet another slap for a job well done.

---

[55] Guidance Enhanced Missile, with improved fusing and better target detection.

There was even talk of the Army transferring the Patriot units over to their service, including personnel. Who would have believed that it was possible to become an airman due to lack of interest on the Army's part?

In the end, nothing came of the transfer scheme but the Army was making it hard for us to be enthusiastic about our branch, especially for me, and I WANTED to shoot down aircraft.

I was disappointed that I did not get a Bronze Star. Although associated with valor awards the BSM is actually awarded for either heroic or meritorious achievement. I felt that, given the fact that I was in the lead element not just of the battery but of the battalion and that I had accomplished every task given to me despite lack of maps, an unreliable GPS system and the high operational tempo. People got Bronze Stars for considerably less.

But when a DA638 Recommendation For Award was processed for me I wound up with an Army Commendation Medal, the second-lowest award for merit and one commonly awarded in peacetime. I wouldn't have minded that so much except that there was no other way for a junior officer to be recognized for meritorious service in a combat environment. It's enough to challenge your faith in Meritocracy.[56]

Soon after the return of our equipment I found myself in a "secret" meeting[57] in a small auditorium with other lieutenants being asked whether or not Alpha had performed well. By that time I had compared notes with other officers and we came to the conclusion that the weapon was not practical for use. Its failure to pick up some targets, its ability to pick up targets outside of engagement range and its tendency to misidentify tracks combined to make us all leery of it.

I personally thought that the operating principle that the machine was based on was flawed. In the open desert atmospherics did things to radio waves which sometimes made them travel farther than they normally would. Modifications of avionics by the Iraqis or simple system failures prevented the Alpha from providing the positive ID that was promised.

As I normally did, I sat up front. This was a habit I picked up from Wright State University[58] and one I probably should have dropped when I went back to the Army. When the civilian technician asked several questions about the Alpha I gave several negative answers. No one else really seemed to want to talk

---

[56] Although overall we didn't do too badly: the National Defense Service Medal, the South-West Asia Service Medal, the Kuwait Liberation Medal, (Saudi Arabia) and the Kuwait Liberation Medal (Kuwait). And those were just the ones for showing up!
[57] You probably have no idea how hard it is to organize a secret meeting in the Army.
[58] "Ptooey!"

about it. Finally, the lieutenant colonel who was standing on one side of the stage walked to the center. "Let's just end this now: raise your hands anyone who would NOT go into combat with this weapon system again."

I raised my hand. Then I looked back: no one else was raising their hand. The other lieutenants I had been speaking to, the ones who agreed with me that the Alpha had problems, were all sitting on their hands.

There was a rumor that the lieutenant-colonel who asked the question was going to be the new project officer for Alpha. Everyone else seemed to have heard that rumor except me. No one wanted to cross this man, which left me looking like a "trouble maker."

If I knew that, or at least had been sitting in the back of the room, would I still have raised my hand when he asked the question? Probably. I used to be stupid like that.

With the Cold War over there was a pursuit of a so-called "peace dividend" by slashing military spending. It was clear that Hawk units would be either eliminated or at least transferred over to the National Guard. Patriot battalions were going to be reduced in number, which meant that there were going to be far fewer battery commands and battalion commands for aspiring ADA officers.

There was considerable postwar personnel turbulence in our battalion. The battery commander and the battalion commander of 2-1 ADA moved on to new assignments and some senior lieutenants also moved to new duty positions. I moved up to 2nd AFU platoon leader and got to (finally) fire a Hawk missile. At a drone. During a training exercise. But at least it was something, and I like being in charge of my own missile system.

I also came in 3rd Place in a battalion-wide TCO competition. This was quite a jump, from being last place in an unofficial pistol competition to being one of the top three officers entrusted to operate the missile system.

Unfortunately it was about this time that the U.S. Army instituted "Consideration Of Others" Training. I only went to one of these mandatory gripe sessions. The whole battery was expected to go to a "neutral" location in civilian clothes. I don't remember much, it was all a politically-correct haze. It seems that I remember likening the whole process to a Chinese Communist self-criticism session.[59]

One thing I distinctly remember thinking was that COOT had to be one of the biggest wastes of time the U.S. Army ever instituted... and considering the competition that was saying something.

---

[59] Part of a proven process of brainwashing.

My next assignment was working for the new ADA Branch Chief, Major General John H. Little, as the Assistant Secretary of the General Staff. As staff positions went it wasn't bad and Maj. Gen. Little was a good boss. As a bonus, general staff officers did not have to attend Consideration Of Others Training. However, as much as the glamour and experience of being a member of a general staff was fun, it was becoming clear that I would have a very difficult time finding a battery command, since so many Hawk and Patriot captains would be trying to get these slots.

So I left active duty to work on an academic career. I went back to WSU[60] and earned an MA in History, which came in handy when I got a job as an IMAX projectionist. I rejoined the Ohio National Guard (2nd Battalion, 174th ADA) and got to fire the very last Hawk missile the Army would launch. Somehow, the rumor got out that I was the lieutenant who accidentally fired the missile in Iraq. It DOES sound like something that would happen to me. I should have just taken credit for it. That would have made three missiles I could say I fired.

Hawk was by then relegated to being a National Guard asset. Raytheon tried to sell a Phase IV version but in the post-Cold War-era defense budgets were still being cut and since Hawk didn't even fire missiles during the Gulf War (well, ONE) the Army decided it wasn't needed in the National Guard either.

Too bad. The Phase IV would have included an improved CWAR, an advanced video tracker (which we could have used at night), anti-radiation missile decoys and a robot for reloading the missiles. I would have been happy with just the robot, as reloading the missiles was both difficult and slightly dangerous.

But the elimination of Hawk DID get rid of Alpha as well.

In 1998 I returned to active-duty from the National Guard. By this time I was a captain. Also by this time, the effects of budget cuts and poor morale were taking their toll on Air Defense Artillery. Patriot battalions were rotating ALMOST every six months[61] and personnel attrition was resulting in some batteries being "administratively deactivated." The equipment was there but not the people, which was no doubt a factor in bringing me back.

I went back to 11th ADA Brigade, but this time as a brigade staff officer. Then I went on a little trip to Kuwait as part of Operation Desert Fox[62] and a second little trip on a battalion rotation to Saudi Arabia. Finally, I got a battery command, even if it was a headquarters unit. I eventually got out of Air Defense

---

[60] See note 5.

[61] If they actually rotated for six full months then certain Army policies regarding overseas duty would kick in.

[62] No, Field Marshal Erwin Rommel was not in charge.

Artillery altogether. Once you don't get to push the launch button anymore ADA isn't that much fun.

I wish I could say that Southern Watch and Desert Fox were my last adventures in the Middle East but unfortunately the 9-11 attacks ensured that I would be back. During these trips weird things still seem to happen to me and I try to find the time to do cartoons about them.

This book was a long time in the making. The inspiration for it came from an article I read from a journalism professor while sitting in the Saudi Desert waiting to cross into Iraq. It bemoaned the fact that reporters were not permitted to simply bounce around the battlefield and interview whoever they wanted and report things to the public (and the enemy) willy-nilly. It also implied that the skills of journalists would be required in order to document the conflict for all time: "if journalists don't write the history of Desert Storm, who will?"

I thought at the time about the unmitigated gall it took to write such a thing. WHO will write the story? As if only reporters and news personalities have mastered the art of putting words into sentences, sentences into paragraphs and paragraphs into chapters. Right then and there I was determined to put together a book when I got back.

It started out from the journals I kept during Desert Shield and Desert Storm. Once back in the States I began turning those hastily-written words into a manuscript, typing it during my off-duty time on a Brother word processor and saving it on a 3" disk. I drew cartoons to illustrate it but mostly kept the cartoons I drew while in Saudi Arabia.

I got rejection after rejection from publishers. No one wanted to publish my Desert Storm story. I wound up getting a copy of the manuscript bound into a one-of-a-kind book by a communist sympathizer (honestly, I could not EVEN make this stuff up) and began work on my first published book, On Air Defense, which came out while I was doing my undergraduate work at Wright State University.[63] I later got a second book published called Guerilla Air Defense, about improvised antiaircraft measures. It was fun and all but I had other things going on and once I returned to the Army I couldn't find time to work on another book.

My wife, God Bless Her, has encouraged me to work on getting this book published and finally, after returning from my 5th time in the Middle East, I picked it up again. After 25 years of writing and editing, not to mention publishing cartoons, I am no longer amazed that the original book was not

---

[63] See note 5.

published... now I am amazed that the various book publishers I sent the manuscript to were as polite as they were with their rejection letters.

What was wrong with it? Well, first of all, it was WAAAAAY too long. Let's face it, not everything we did was that interesting. Plus, I left out some things because they were embarrassing at the time, or not releasable (like Alpha). And the cartoons I drew had the kernel of a good idea but with only one or two exceptions were badly executed. After all, I was using army-issue tube markers when I could get them and whatever I could find for paper.

Was the book salvageable? Having helped other people with manuscripts I thought so, and began working on it. The original journals are missing and the disk I stored the manuscript on is gone (and I got rid of my Brother word-processor some time back) so I reviewed the bound copy page by page and retyped it. I deleted as I went along. I added some new material. And I also took the time to redo the illustrations and cartoons so they are not just better quality but also consistent with one another.

And there was the whole issue of getting the Army to admit that Alpha existed. Having been published before I knew the procedure one had to follow in order for a service member to get permission to print. Nevertheless, I was sent from the OCPA-NY office to XVIII Airborne Corps G-2 to CENTCOM FOIA Office to the DA FOIA Office to Army G-2 to the Office of the Chief of Public Affairs, all in an effort to make sure this book can be *legally* published. It's hard not to get frustrated at how the various offices of the Army can explain to you why THEY don't handle "this sort of thing" while they refer you to someone else... who doesn't handle this sort of thing either.

The fact that you are reading this is a victory of individual perseverance over bureaucracy.

Eventually, the mural highlighting 11th ADA Brigade's role in Desert Storm was painted over at the Officer's Club. Scud pieces which once were once part of office decorations were put away and forgotten. The launch dates on the Patriot launchers were covered over. The scudbuster souvenirs went away. The Air Defense Artillery Center was deactivated and its functions transferred to Fort Sill, Oklahoma. Patriot's tarnished reputation became just another casualty of Desert Storm.

13. ONE MORE THING

In retrospect, it's probably just as well I didn't get to shoot down an enemy aircraft. The paperwork would have been HORRENDOUS.

Speaking of paperwork, I found something interesting while going through some old papers. I have given up getting any company to admit to having knowledge of the Alpha System. But I found a form for some training on Hawk that I couldn't remember. When I looked at it the date I realized that it was to certify that I had trained up on the Hawk IIIA, even though this form doesn't mention it by name.

So I guess I'm NOT crazy. At least when it comes to missile systems.

APPENDIX 1: GLOSSARY OF TERMS AND ACRONYMS

AAA- Anti-Aircraft Artillery; collective term for guns employed to shoot down airplanes.

ADA- Air Defense Artillery, a branch of the United States Army, on par with Infantry or Cavalry.

ADP- Automatic Data Processor, the computer used by Phase III Hawk.

AFP- Assault Fire Platoon, the smallest Army element equipped with the Hawk Missile System. A Phase III Hawk Battery had two: AFP I and AFP II.

AFN- Armed Forces Network, the military's own radio and TV network.

ALPHA- a passive air defense weapon system capable of identifying specific aircraft types. Official designation: Hawk IIIA.

ARM- Anti-Radiation Missile, an air-launched weapon designed to home in on and destroy the radars of surface-to-air missile systems.

AWACS- Airborne Warning and Control System, an airplane used to detect and track enemy aircraft and to direct friendly interceptors and other air defense assets against the enemy. The E-3 Sentry was the designation of the actual AWACS airplane.

BC- Battery Commander.

BCC- Battery Command Central, an obsolete piece of equipment used in Hawk I and II.

CO- Commanding Officer.

CP- Command Post. A van or building used for unit administration and staff work.

CUCV- Commercial Utility Cargo Vehicle; normally pronounced as "cutvee."

CWAR- Continuous-Wave Acquisition Radar, the part of the Hawk missile system which detects enemy aircraft at longer ranges.

DCU- Desert Camouflage Uniform, a desert version of the Battle Dress Uniform worn by the U.S. Army at the time.

ECM- Electronic Counter-Measures, methods used to fool or confuse radar in order to prevent enemy weapon engagement. This can include jamming, chaff or spoofing.

ECCM- Electronic Counter-Counter-Measures, methods used to negate the ECM being used to fool or confuse the radar and to allow weapon engagement. This can include frequency shifting, the use of additional radar assets and employment of high energy to "burn" through jamming.

ECCCM- Electronic Counter-Counter-Counter Measures, measures used to overcome ECCM.

EPW- Enemy Prisoner of War.

GCI- Ground Controlled Interception, a rigid Soviet-style method of directing fighters.

GPS- Global Positioning System.

HAWK- a surface-to-air missile system employed by the United States Army to defend the Army and key assets against air attack. Although not officially an acronym, HAWK is said to stand for Homing All the Way Killer, a reflection of its method of engaging enemy aircraft. It has also been called a Holiday And Weekend Killer, a reflection of its habit of breaking down right when you expect to get off work.

HIMAD- High-to-Medium Air Defense; those air defense weapons capable of tracking and engaging enemy aircraft at surprising (for the enemy) distances. Hawk and Patriot are HIMAD systems.

HMMWV- High Mobility Multipurpose Wheeled Vehicle, an Army utility vehicle. Commonly pronounced "humvee."

HPIR- High-Power Illuminating Radar, the Hawk's targeting radar.

ICC- Information Coordination Central, A Patriot battalion-level control van which could also control Hawk batteries.

IFF- Identification Friend or Foe, the electronic coded signal-and-reply system used to tell friendly aircraft from enemy.

IQAF- Iraqi Air Force (as used at the time).

J-Box- Junction Box, used to control electronic access to Hawk missiles.

KKMC- King Khalid Military City. Sometimes called the Emerald City due to a large, ornate green building in the heart of the base. Home of the 11th ADA Brigade TOC during Desert Storm.

KSA- Kingdom of Saudi Arabia. Sometimes called the Magic Kingdom.

LASHE- Low-Altitude Simultaneous Hawk Engagement. This type of engagement employs a special antenna attached to the HIPIR to send out a fan rather than a narrow beam, thus illuminating several targets simultaneously instead of individually. This allows the rapid fire of Hawk missiles to defeat a saturation attack. It has two drawbacks: the range is closer and rapidly firing the missiles can result in rapidly running out of missiles.

LBE- Load-Bearing Equipment; this is a belt-and-strap system which allows a soldier to carry his canteen, ammunition, first-aid kit, etc. And still have his hands free to shoot things.

MEZ- Missile Engagement Zone, a volume of airspace in which SAMs enforce the "do not enter" status.

MiG- A Russian acronym which stands for Mikoyan-Gurevich, a design bureau which lends its name to many Soviet (and now Russian) fighter aircraft. Once a common designation for any high-speed Soviet aircraft, regardless of whether it was designed and produced by MiG, Sukhoi, Yakovlev or Tupolev.

MIGCAP- A Combat Air Patrol directed at intercepting the enemy, who will presumably be flying MiGs.

MLRS- Multiple-Launch Rocket System.

MOPP- Mission-Oriented Protective Posture, a system of protective overgarments, gloves, overboots and mask designed to protect the wearer from chemical, biological and nuclear weapons. The level is adjusted according to the likelihood of attack and the nature of possible attack.

MRE- Meals, Ready to Eat.

MSR- Main Supply Route; Two key ones for us were MSR Dodge (Tapline Road) and MSR Texas.

MWO- Movement Warning Order; instructions to relocate.

NET- Usually refers to the air defense network of radars, weapons and communications links protecting the Coalition.

NCO- Non-Commissioned Officer, almost always a sergeant of some stripe or other.

PADS- Position and Azimuth Determining System, a vehicle-mounted electronic surveying system which depends on inertial measurements to provide location and elevation. During Desert Storm the only PADS teams we knew of were associated with Patriot.

PAR- Pulse Acquisition Radar, a long-range radar used to acquire targets for Hawk.

PATRIOT- A surface-to-air missile system employed by the United States Army to defend the Army and key assets against air and missile attack. Extensively used during Desert Storm to intercept Iraqi Scuds and at the time the only SAM system capable of intercepting such missiles.

PCP- Platoon Command Post, the control van for a Hawk AFP and where you would find the TCO and RO.

POW- Prisoner of War; used to refer to one of OUR people who got captured.

PT- Physical Training; in the Army context this almost always ends up having something to do with running.

RO- Radar Operator, the enlisted soldier who assists the TCO in operating the Hawk missile system. Listens and evaluates the return signal from the HIPIR.

ROR- Range Only Radar, a radar used in older versions of Hawk to initiate ECCM.

RPG- Rocket-Propelled Grenade, a weapon devised by the Soviets for knocking out vehicles and bunkers and exported to their subsidiaries throughout the world.

RSOP- Reconnaissance, Selection and Occupation of Position; RSOP Teams are responsible for scouting future positions for HIMAD units.

SAM- Surface-to-Air Missile.

SCUD- a generic term for an SS-1 surface-to-surface missile, a modified SS-1 or a variant of the SS-1. Extensively used by Saddam during Desert Storm.

SHORAD- Short-Range Air Defense, very often a term for those ADA weapons which required the use of eyeballs for target detection and engagement. Stinger and Avenger are SHORAD weapons.

SLGR- Small Lightweight GPS Receiver, a hand-held 1st generation GPS used by the Army during Desert Shield/Storm.

TAS- Tracking Adjunct System, a video camera system mounted on the HIPIR which permitted passive tracking of targets by Hawk. Passively tracking the target permitted the operator to switch to active tracking when the reaction time would be minimal to the pilot.

TBM- Tactical Ballistic Missile, usually a reference to a so-called "battlefield" missile. A Scud is an example of a TBM, although its use in Desert Storm was meant to be strategic.

TCO- Tactical Control Officer, a duty position in a Hawk fire unit. The TCO tracks and launches missiles at enemy aircraft.

TD- Tactical Director, a duty position in a Hawk battalion. The TD sets priorities for the fire units, passes down warnings and effectively sets the rules of engagement.

TOC- Tactical Operations Center, a command-and-control center, either a set of vans in the field or a building in a built-up area, linked by radio and data systems in order to provide guidance to units.

Transloader- a HAWK transporter/loader vehicle. This machine could carry and load up to three missiles simultaneously.

USAF- United States Air Force.

Vu-Graph- a primitive briefing system in which information was printed on clear 8x12" slides and projected on a movie-type screen. Slides were changed (or "flipped") by hand. This was the predecessor to Powerpoint.

Wild Weasel- term for aircraft and aircrew especially trained and equipped to destroy enemy air defenses.

APPENDIX 2: A SHORT HISTORY OF SECRET WEAPONS

The term "secret weapon" often stirs up images of mad scientists and huge, deadly and unstoppable machines in the popular imagination, thanks to popular literature and Hollywood. The actual history of secret weapons is a little more mundane.

WHY are secret weapons kept secret? Sometimes it is because the weapon employs some new line of technological development, one that the enemy might exploit themselves if they knew about it. Sometimes it is because secrecy leads to an even greater impact on the enemy when it is finally used. Sometimes it is a matter of both.

The Trojan Horse can be looked upon as the earliest secret weapon. The Trojan Horse was actually a big, wooden *Greek* horse, left outside the walls of the city of Troy after a long siege by the Greeks failed to get the Trojans to surrender. With the Greek force gone from the beach the Trojans wheeled the wooden beast inside the walls of their city, taking it as a war trophy. They didn't realize that the hollow statue contained a crack commando team of Greek hoplites.

That night the Greeks descended from the Trojan Horse and secured and opened the gates of the city, thus ending the war. This was before the days when reporters found it necessary to tell everyone what their own side intended to do to the enemy, so secrecy insured success. Even so, there was no technological component to this "weapon" and indeed the horse was used to take advantage of a tactical surprise.

Greek Fire is one of the earliest examples of a secret weapon, as the term is understood today. The Byzantine Empire used this incendiary to attack enemy ships... it was a burning liquid which floated on water. The Byzantines had special delivery systems to use the weapon against enemy ships, such as cranes for pouring it onto an enemy ship some distance from their own vessels and even grenades and a kind of primitive flamethrower for ground troops. The Byzantine Empire, armed with Greek Fire, managed to survive the fall of the Western Roman Empire to the Germanic barbarians and to hold off the Muslim empires which made encroachments to their territory over a period of 500 years.

The formula for Greek Fire was a closely guarded military secret. While there is a lot of historical conjecture about what actually went into the weapon no reliable formula has ever been found and no chemical concoction whipped up by modern scientists has ever managed to reproduce the same effects attributed to Greek Fire. The secret died with the Byzantine Empire. This proves that secret weapons aren't always game changers and that it IS possible to keep a military secret indefinitely.

During the Civil War there were a lot of new weapons developed, but the principles or tactics involved with them were already known: armored naval vessels, breech-loading guns, railroad guns. However, at the end of 1864 the Union forces tried a new weapon: a bomb ship.

This was simply a steamship which was packed with nothing but explosives. The intention was to use explode the ship in the middle of the night near Fort Fisher, a key Confederate installation. The sheer size of the explosion was believed to be capable of severely damaging the fortress walls, unseating several large artillery pieces and allowing the Yankees to take the fort with an amphibious landing.

The ship was moored in the darkness near the fort by a volunteer skeleton crew and an elaborate detonating system set up to ensure the gun powder would all blow up at the same time. While the bomb ship DID result in the largest man-made explosion to that time, it was not close enough to cause significant damage to the fort. It did wake up the garrison in time for them to prepare for the amphibious landing of Union troops, however.

In the 1860s the French developed the Mitrailleuse, an automatic weapon capable of firing 100 rounds a minute. It had a range of up to 2000 yards, placing it outside the reach of the "needle gun," the firearm of choice for the Prussian army. The French was equipped with over 200 of these weapons when the Franco-Prussian War broke out in 1870.

Unfortunately for the French, the weapon was kept such a great secret that most of the French generals fighting the war never saw one until it was wheeled past them on the way to the battlefield. When this predecessor to the machinegun was figured out by the officers they employed it the same way they would artillery (the weapon did somewhat resemble an artillery piece) instead of using it to support the infantry. After the French lost the war the Mitrailleuse was phased out of the army.

During World War I the Germans developed a secret weapon in the form of a long-range gun. This huge cannon was built for the sole purpose of bombarding strategic targets, rather than providing tactical support. The gun fired a 234-pound shell over 81 miles away and the projectile was the first man-made object to enter the stratosphere, reaching an altitude of over 26 miles. The range and altitude was so great that the rotation of the earth had to be calculated into the firing data.

The weapon had its problems, though. Despite the best efforts of the gunners, the Paris Gun was not very accurate: it needed an entire city for a target. Despite this weakness, the Germans hoped that the weapon might serve as a psyops weapon, demoralizing the French populace of Paris.

The weapon came too late in the war, during the last year. The German Army was already on the ropes and the gun was withdrawn as the Allies began their last push. The weapon disappeared, probably dismantled, as the Armistice was drawn up to demilitarize the new German Republic. Even the plans for the gun have never been located. Like Greek Fire, the secrets of the Paris Gun disappeared with the empire that spawned it.

World War II was the Golden Age of Secret Weapons. There was hardly a major power which did not have one in the works, from flying tanks to the atomic bomb. Some proved to be successful and even adopted as conventional weapons after the war while others were failures or never got past the prototype stage.

Everyone has heard of the atomic bomb, a weapon so secret that it was even hidden from the vice-president of the United States, but few have heard of the Bat Bomb. The Bat Bomb was based upon the fact that Japanese cities were almost entirely wood-and-paper constructs. This was combined with the fact that bats like to hang under the eaves of buildings during the day. These two ideas were combined to arm bats with incendiary devices. The bats were to be delivered by bombs which would release the bats before reaching the ground. The devices would go off after the bats had enough time to get comfortable under the roofs of vulnerable buildings. The ASPCA was not consulted by the War Department when this weapon was invented.

While being perfected bats armed with the incendiaries were accidentally released and as a result an Army airfield in Carlsbad New Mexico suffered severe fire damage. The project was then handed over to the Navy. Later, they decided to hand it over to the Marines. Finally, the project was scrapped altogether. It is notable that Soviet spies never tried to steal THIS particular secret weapon.

On the Eastern Front the Red Army fielded the BM-13 Stalin Organ. This alternative to regular artillery employed a barrage of shrieking rockets towards the enemy and had a bigger psychological impact than the inaccurate missiles warranted. The sound the BM-13 made, along with its general appearance when loaded, contributed to the nickname given to it by the Germans.

Initially the Stalin Organ was operated by the NKVD to keep it a secret, probably with the understanding that the chekists would shoot THEMSELVES for a change if they revealed the weapon's existence. Later in the war the secret was out and the NKVD went back to operating prison camps and penal battalions.

Japan, which lacked the industrial base to match the United States when it came to aircraft production, came up with what would appear to be a step backwards in military technology: balloon bombs. These balloons (called Fu-Go by the Japanese) were launched from Japan and were carried on the jet stream to western Canada and the United States. These balloons carried one of three payloads: high-explosives, incendiaries or a radio tracking package. Explosives or incendiaries would be released by a timing mechanism while the radio tracker provided the Japanese with some idea of how far the bombs were going.

The bombs did cause some fires but the most dangerous part of this program was the intention to mate the balloons with biological weapons, which might have caused significant casualties if used. However, the Japanese had no confirmation that the bombs were causing forest fires or blowing up random locations because the U.S. Army was already aware that these bombs were coming over and had taken appropriate steps to both intercept the balloons and to censor newspapers from reporting incidents which would have encouraged the Japanese to launch more such attacks.

Germany had probably more secret weapons in the works per-capita than any other belligerent in WWII. One stands out, and that was the Maus.

During the war tanks kept getting bigger and bigger and more heavily armed. The Maus was meant to jump ahead of this curve by simply making the biggest, most powerful tank in the world.

It sounded impressive: a tank with a 137mm gun (the biggest at the time was 88mm) with a coaxial 75mm gun (many tanks didn't have a gun that big for its primary armament!). The problem was that the thing was so heavy (200 tons) that the best engine could barely make it crawl at 12 mph.

The Maus was hardly a Blitzkrieg weapon and production would have crippled Germany's ability to build smaller, but still lethal, tanks.

After WWII the effectiveness of conventional weapons was at an all-time high, not to mention there were large numbers of such weapons, so the need for secret weapons waned. Some secrecy was maintained when it came to variations of different atomic weapons but that had more to do with keeping them secure than with keeping their existence (or operating principal) secret. Rogue states like North Korea worked secretly on semi-submersibles and longer-range missiles, but these were variations on known principles.

There were one or two exceptional developments during this period, however. One was the development of stealth aircraft by the U.S. Air Force. These airplanes are not particularly fast or could fly very high, but because of new materials and design they are very hard to pick up on radar and could therefore hit an enemy who expected to have some kind of warning before the enemy showed up.

Another was the supergun, a cannon designed by Dr. Gerald Bull. Inspired by Germany's Paris Cannon and having done some work for NASA on a project called HARP, Bull was willing to sell Saddam Hussein a weapon that, in theory, could hit Israel from Iraqi territory. The secrecy surrounding this project was blown prior to the Persian Gulf War and the shipment of at least some of the components under construction in Europe were impounded on their way to Iraq.

So, secrecy and weapons go hand in hand. Secrecy can be overdone and weapons which might make a difference are not there when they are needed. Other secret weapons might never have been pursued if someone in authority but outside the circle of secrecy could have pointed out flaws to the operating principle involved or questioned the need for it. And yet others required secrecy to be effective. Without it their effectiveness was either severely limited (as in the case of stealth aircraft) or absent altogether (such as in the case of the Alpha).

APPENDIX 3: HANGFIRES, MISFIRES AND DUDS

If you've ever watched the Roadrunner cartoons and elaborate booby traps and fantastic weaponry brought to bear by Wile E. Coyote to destroy that bird, then you might be forgiven for thinking that the military science of ground-pounders trying to eliminate the airborne foe is far more sophisticated. The historical truth is, regardless of how far we have come, some strange ideas right out of *Looney Toons* have been brought to bear in an effort to shoot down aircraft.

During World War I a new problem came along for soldiers to deal with. In addition to bugs, mud, artillery barrages, nasty food and nastier generals (it didn't matter who's) the doughboy of the Great War had to deal with aero planes. Initially the canvas-and-wood aircraft were just a nuisance, scouting around the battlefield. This was bad news, but something that could be dealt with. Then they began directing artillery fire. This was VERY bad news and enough to get the attention of the brass several miles to the rear of the lines. By the time the American Expeditionary Force arrived "Over There" the flyboys had graduated to dropping bombs on enemy troops and even using their machine guns to strafe trenches.

Someone got the idea to take an ordinary cannon and rig them up to point at its airborne target. But how to aim it? The unofficial M1 Antiaircraft Gun Sight consisted of a bottle opener with vertical and horizontal strings across the open end forming crosshairs.

These jerry-rigged antiaircraft guns were less notable for their accuracy (2500-3000 rounds on average to bring down an airplane) than for their nuisance value. How seriously the Red baron could take someone aiming at him with one hand while holding an open bottle with the other is anyone's guess.

When Japan became involved in the Pacific War their ground-based air defenses got very low priority when it came to military spending. Tokyo figured "Why worry about air attack? Don't we have an ocean to protect us?" They should have paid more attention: that was the same mindset we had when Pearl Harbor took place.

Following the Doolittle Raid it rapidly became obvious that the "What Me Worry?" approach to antiaircraft was totally wrong and that it might be a good idea to get some weapons to shoot down the "Yankee air pirates" who were making an appearance over the many islands of the Greater East Asia Co-Prosperity Sphere. In addition to conventional antiaircraft artillery and automatic weapons the Japanese developed a unique new weapon: the barrage mortar.

The "system" utilized individual mortars, each one consisting of a tube on a spiked wooden base, and a specialized mortar shell. The 70mm and 81mm versions had no aiming equipment, no specialized gunsight, no settings... it was simply planted in the ground with the tube aimed upwards. When an enemy aircraft approached the shells were rapidly fed into the tube, and immediately traveled upwards to an altitude of 1,700 feet. The shells would deploy small charges on parachutes and in theory provided a small cloud of deadly airborne mines ready to explode as soon as an aircraft touched the cord holding the parachute.

There were many drawbacks to this attempt to provide a dedicated man-portable air defense system. First, it was based on the principle of using a barrage, or a large number of shells to create a formidable airborne barrier to enemy planes. One mortar, even one that deploys several smaller charges and has an enthusiastic gunner dropping rounds as quickly as he can, cannot keep enough charges in the air to make up for the lack of accuracy of the weapon... the law of averages was definitely with the pilot in this case. Even if the pilot was being particularly unlucky enough to hit a cord and set off the charge it was so small that was unlikely to cause critical damage.

This made the barrage mortar almost totally ineffective as an air defense system. It could neither destroy aircraft nor provide a deterrence effect... most pilots never realized they were being targeted by antiaircraft fire! Meanwhile, the charges were very much active all the way to the ground... which made their use very hard indeed on friendly troops who happened to be downwind of the barrage.

A similar weapon was tried by the British in the early days of WWII, before Winston Churchill took on the job of Prime Minister. As First Lord of the Admiralty he came up with the idea of "aerial minefields;" these were created by mass-firing rockets from deck-mounted projectors, with each rocket distributing a number of mines connected by wire to parachutes. In theory, the Naval Wire System (NWS) put many aerial obstacles in the path of aircraft attempting to attack convoys, especially if each ship had at least one projector.

In practice it was found that the mines tended to land on the decks of the very same ships they were meant to protect, or worse become ensnared via their wires in the superstructure and antennas. This system was retired as soon as more conventional weapons were available.

Germany, as with so many military projects, looked to employ an unexplored principle to build an antiaircraft weapon that needed no ammunition. This was the Wind Gun and it was designed to use compressed air to destroy enemy aircraft. Using a controlled explosion of oxygen and hydrogen the Wind Gun "fired" a dense plug of air at its target. German scientists believed that the plug would cause critical damage to high-flying Allied bombers but the plug would begin to dissipate upon firing and could barely break boards at ranges of a few hundred meters during test trials.

So desperate was Germany's military situation, however, that the system was deployed on the Eastern Front, protecting a bridge from air attack even as the Red Army closed in on Berlin. There is no record of its use in either side's reports: the Germans probably never filed one out of embarrassment and the Soviets never filed one because they probably didn't realize the ungainly machine was a weapon.

One of the major air defense problems identified during World War II was the need for a gun system to cover the "dead zone," the area between the lower effective altitude covered by heavy antiaircraft guns like the German 8,8cm and the highest altitude reached by automatic weapons like the Quad .50 machine gun. By the end of the war there was no satisfactory solution but in the case of the British 57mm gun it wasn't for lack of trying.

The gun, also known as the 6pdr 6cwt when it is known at all, has to be the ultimate example of an air defense weapon designed by committee. It had a dozen different versions, including an anti-motorboat version, a variant equipped with an automatic loading system (which was bigger than the gun it serviced), and a rapid-traverse model (which had a tendency to get stuck a lot and was deemed less reliable than the manual-traverse version), as well as Sprung, Partially Sprung, and Unsprung versions.

Having various models of a weapon is, in itself, not unusual but in this case not a single variant ever made it to combat. Every time the Good Idea Fairy added a change the production line had to be held up while everything was retooled. To add insult to injury the gun was declared obsolete in 1948, never having engaged a target.

The Soviets were always rather secretive about military technology... at least until May Day, and even then there were no programs handed out identifying the latest ICBM model being driven down Red Square or what the designation of the new bomber flying overhead was. Therefore it is not surprising that we in the West had little or no information about an antiaircraft missile we called the Griffon.

The missile was considered a disaster by STAVKA, although we can't be sure of exactly why, given the Soviet reluctance to admit failure (see "Chenobyl

Brand Glow-in-the-Dark Watches" ad campaign), but this lack of information allows us to speculate. Perhaps the a Griffon missile strayed off course during a test and destroyed the Third Patriotic Peasants and Workers Grenade Factory, or perhaps it turned out that the missile system's alcohol-based fuel was too great a temptation for its crews and they were routinely higher than their under-fueled rockets.

In any case, the weapon was only deployed to one city, Leningrad, and an effort was made to dismantle the missile bunkers only a few years after they were built. The Griffon's radar appears never to have been installed at all. Within a short time the entire system had been eliminated with an eagerness that the Soviets seem to reserve for weapon systems which are obsolete or designed by a known "enemy of the people.'

The concept of the Sergeant York Gun was sound enough: provide the U.S. Army with a gun system which can keep up with the armored columns and finally replace the Chaparral and Vulcan air defense systems, which had been brought into service on a temporary basis to provide low-level air defense. But from that sound idea came mistakes which did for Air Defense Artillery what Three Mile Island did for the nuclear energy industry.

Ford Aerospace won the Army's DIVAD (Divisional Air Defense) competition for the new gun system by creating a hybrid: a Swedish L/70 40mm gun carried by an M48 tank chassis and aimed by a radar used on the F-16. It was hoped that by using "off-the-shelf" components that the weapon system would be cheaper to produce and maintain, especially since M48 tanks were to be replaced with M1 tanks, thus freeing up a lot of previously-used M48s which could be converted to Sergeant York Guns.

That SOUNDS smart until you look at it closer. The reason M48 Patton tanks were being replaced was because the M1 tank was *faster*. If the Sergeant York Gun had to keep up with the armored columns it was going about it the wrong way. Also, the components had been developed for different environments (the radar for airborne use, the tank for ground travel, etc.) and had serious teething problems. In one case, the electronics shorted out when the Sergeant York was washed ("That's OK, it doesn't rain in the desert."). In another it locked onto a latrine ventilation fan by mistake during gun trials (the computer classified the latrine as a "low priority" target). But the worst problem was that the system had difficulty "seeing" helicopters, the biggest threat the Sergeant York was designed for... the Doppler radar picked up the speed of a blade heading towards it and the speed of another heading away from it, subtracted one from the other and came up with zero... no target.

Even though the German Gepard and the Soviet Shilka (both contemporaries of the Sergeant York) proved that the battlefield air defense gun system could work, the Sergeant York gun simply couldn't meet the needs of the Army. This was really brought home when the USSR began equipping its Hind-D helicopters with AT-6 missiles... which had a range of 6 kilometers. With a 4 kilometer range the Sergeant York was outmatched. By the time Desert Storm came along the few production models were in storage or on their way to museums.

To expect no mistakes in the development of air defense weapons would be the height of folly... air defense is one of the most complex and challenge fields of military science. It is natural that some mistakes will be made while new and better ways of destroying enemy aircraft are devised. The true folly would be in failing to learn from our mistakes.

(Originally published in the July-August 1990 issue of Air Defense Artillery Magazine; article by James D. Crabtree, artwork by Dennis Kurtz)

INDEX

James "Doc" Crabtree began his Army career in 1982 as a Hawk surface-to-air missile crewman and was later retrained to take his place in one of the first Patriot units then being formed. He applied to go to West Point Preparatory School (which was lost) and later applied for an Active-Duty ROTC Scholarship (which arrived AFTER he left the Army at the completion of his enlistment).

Crabtree was commissioned in 1989 and was placed back on active duty just in time for Operation Desert Shield in Saudi Arabia. He served as a Tactical Control Officer for a Hawk battery and operated a secret weapon attached to the Hawk called "Alpha." All efforts to get Hughes Aircraft to admit they built this thing (it had their name stamped on the components) have been fruitless.

When Desert Storm concluded Crabtree found himself in southern Iraq.

Following Gulf War I Doc Crabtree went to Ohio to get a graduate degree in history and worked for a time at the U.S. Air Force Museum. During this period he wrote *On Air Defense* and *Guerrilla Air Defense.* He was asked to return to active duty in 1998 just in time to take part in Operation Desert Fox, which gave him the opportunity to visit Kuwait for the first time. Within a year he was off again, this time back to Saudi Arabia as part of Operation Southern Watch.

In 2003 Crabtree became a Public Affairs Officer and found himself in Iraq in 2005. The only time he was ever shot at was while he was serving in the U.S. Army as a PAO.

Doc Crabtree's next overseas assignment was in the Sinai, where he saw signs of the security situation there spinning out of control. He next went to Guantanamo Bay, where his detachment took care the pitifully few reporters interested in going to the detention facility following the election of President Obama.

Throughout his Army career Doc Crabtree has enjoyed drawing cartoons and has written for Army publications. In addition to his first five books (one of which was found in bin Laden's "library" during the raid that killed him) Crabtree intends to publish a book on the detention facility at Guantanamo Bay and how the media loved to hate it until President Obama was elected.

Found in bin Laden's compound during the raid that killed him, Guerrilla Air Defense broke ground at the time of its publication in the 1990s as the ONLY book on improvised air defense. Now it is available again, with revamped illustrations and a look at new aerial threats, such as killer drones. Only air defense historian Doc Crabtree could tell this story.

Now available on Amazon.com.

"Fatalistic, SNAFU-fueled humor which should be instantly recognizable if you've ever known anybody who has served in the military."

-Goodreads Reviewer

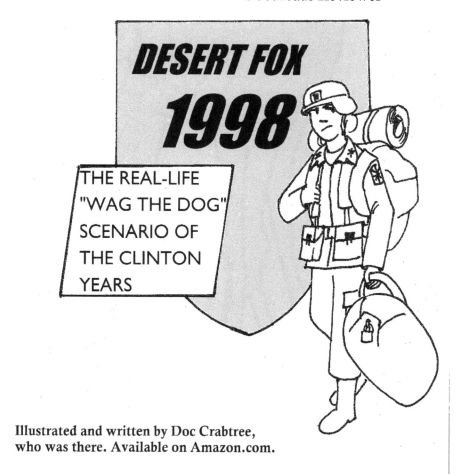

DESERT FOX

1998

THE REAL-LIFE "WAG THE DOG" SCENARIO OF THE CLINTON YEARS

Illustrated and written by Doc Crabtree, who was there. Available on Amazon.com.

"Who knew peacekeeping could be this funny?"

*Available on
Amazon.com!*

ORANGE BERETS
ADVENTURES AND MISADVENTURES
IN THE SINAI

CPSIA information can be obtained
at www.ICGtesting.com
Printed in the USA
LVHW030859040520
654932LV00005B/1451